BLOOD AND GOLD

THE AMERICAS AT WAR

Written by Graham Briggs, Richard Bodley
Scott & Rudy Scott Nelson, assisted by
Nik Gaukroger, James Hamilton and
Paul Robinson

OSPREY
PUBLISHING

SLITHERINE

First published in Great Britain in 2009 by Osprey Publishing Ltd.
© 2009 Osprey Publishing Ltd and Slitherine Software UK Ltd.

Osprey Publishing, Midland House, West Way, Botley, Oxford OX2 0PH, UK
443 Park Avenue South, New York, NY 10016, USA

E-mail: info@ospreypublishing.com

Slitherine Software UK Ltd., The White Cottage, 8 West Hill Avenue, Epsom, KT 19 8LE, UK
E-mail: info@slitherine.co.uk

A CIP catalogue record for this book is available from the British Library

ISBN: 978 1 84603 691 0
E-book ISBN: 978 1 84908 135 1

Rules system by Richard Bodley Scott, Simon Hall and Terry Shaw
Page layout and cover concept by Myriam Bell Design, France
Index by Mike Parkin
Typeset in Joanna Pro and Sleepy Hollow
Cover artwork by Peter Dennis
Photography by Eureka Miniatures, Outpost Wargame Services, Paul Hannah, Richard Woolford, Steve Price
& Bear's Den Miniatures
All artwork and cartography © Osprey Publishing Ltd
Project management by JD McNeil and Osprey Team
Technical management by Iain McNeil
Originated by PDQ Media, Bungay, UK
Printed in China through Worldprint Ltd

09 10 11 12 13   10 9 8 7 6 5 4 3 2 1

FOR A CATALOGUE OF ALL BOOKS PUBLISHED BY OSPREY MILITARY AND AVIATION
PLEASE CONTACT:

NORTH AMERICA
Osprey Direct, c/o Random House Distribution Center, 400 Hahn Road, Westminster, MD 21157
E-mail: uscustomerservice@ospreypublishing.com

ALL OTHER REGIONS
Osprey Direct, The Book Service Ltd, Distribution Centre, Colchester Road,
Frating Green, Colchester, Essex, CO7 7DW
E-mail: customerservice@ospreypublishing.com

FOR DETAILS OF ALL GAMES PUBLISHED BY SLITHERINE SOFTWARE UK LTD
E-mail: info@slitherine.co.uk

Osprey Publishing is supporting the Woodland Trust, the UK's leading woodland
conservation charity, by funding the dedication of trees.

www.ospreypublishing.com
www.slitherine.com

CONTENTS

INTRODUCTION

This book covers the armies of the Pre-Columbian Americas until shortly before the arrival of the Spanish conquistadors in the early 16th century AD.

In Pre-Columbian America there were no horses and wheeled vehicles were unknown. Nevertheless, a series of sophisticated civilisations arose which built cities that outshone their contemporaries in Europe. Despite the lack of iron tools, impressive architecture was created, intensive agricultural systems were developed and the Incas built a remarkably extensive road system.

On the other hand, the practice of human sacrifice was common to many of the Pre-Columbian religions, including those of the Maya, Aztecs and Incas. The Aztecs were said to have sacrificed between 20,000 and 50,000 people per year, by cutting out their still-beating hearts. Their whole system of warfare came to be dominated by the need to acquire prisoners for sacrifice. At the re-consecration of the great temple in Tenochtitlan in 1488, according to differing accounts, between 4,000 and 80,400 people were sacrificed over a period of four days.

The Maya had a written language, as did the Aztecs. Unfortunately, the Spanish conquistadors burned most of the pre-conquest Aztec writings. However, following a change of heart by the conquerors, Spanish-trained native scribes were able to document the Aztec way of life in Codices such as the Codex Mendoza, while there was

Skull Racks

Mexica Emperor and attendants, by Angus McBride. Taken from Men-at-Arms 239: Aztec, Mixtec and Zapotec Armies.

still living memory. These books, written in a combination of Aztec glyphs and Spanish, contain all the information we have on military training, promotion, tribute, campaign histories and the various ranks of warrior. There is also a great deal of archaeological evidence. However, much of what we know about Pre-Columbian warfare comes from descriptions given by the Spanish conquistadors and other European colonists of the 16th century, after the end of our period.

The Incas had developed a form of bronze, but in much of South America and in Meso- and North America, weapons were of wood or stone (or fish or animal teeth or bone). These materials were sometimes combined in sophisticated ways – such as the wooden swords with razor-sharp edges made of obsidian (volcanic glass) used by

the Aztecs and others. Many of the hand-to-hand weapons inflicted horrific injuries. Most were more suited to crushing or cutting actions rather than thrusting.

We have been fairly generous in granting Swordsmen capability to some warriors armed only with short clubs for close combat. However Swordsmen capability is as much about attitude to and experience of close combat as it is about specific weaponry. We have adopted the same general approach in our other *Field of Glory* Companions.

Armour, where used, was usually designed to protect the head and torso from crushing and cutting blows and was made of thick layers of plant fibres – cotton and maguey being common and some areas using wooden armour. These

The Great Temple at Tenochtitlan

armours were often covered with bright feather work, at least for the more esteemed warriors. Shields were frequently of the parrying type, although large solid shields are known.

Missile weapons included slings, throwing spears, bolas and bows.

The atlatl was a device for throwing short spears further and with more penetration than was possible by hand. It consisted of a grooved shaft with a cup or a spur at the end to retain the butt of the projectile until the moment of launch. Modern tests have achieved ranges of greater than 100 metres and speeds of over 150 km/h. The atlatl gradually came to be replaced by the bow, which had the advantage of greater range and of permitting the effective use of lighter missiles – allowing more to be carried. However, the atlatl was still in extensive use in Mesoamerica at the time of the Spanish conquest in the 16th century.

Spanish sources describe a heavy barrage of atlatl darts prior to close combat. In view of their extra range and penetrative power compared with javelins or darts thrown without the aid of an atlatl, we give Medium Foot equipped with atlatl Javelins shooting capability as well as including the effect of atlatl darts in their Impact Phase capability.

Logistics tended to be a major challenge, as in many armies everything had to be carried by porters, and roads were relatively poor. This meant that large scale empires were the exception rather than the rule as few states had the reach to quell rebellious distant provinces. The Incas were an exception, having llamas available as pack-animals, and a well-developed Imperial road system. These allowed them to extend their conquests to encompass a swathe of territory an astonishing 5,000 kilometres (3,000 miles) in north-south length, much of it steeply mountainous.

Mayan Warrior with atlatl

OLMEC

The Olmecs were the first substantial civilization in Central America. Their heartland was the Gulf Coast of Mexico, corresponding with the modern Mexican states of Tabasco and Veracruz. They built major centres at San Lorenzo, Tenochtitlan, La Venta and Tres Zapotes and farmed the rich alluvial soils of the coastal rivers. Their influence spread as far as modern-day Guatemala, supported by a trade in jade and obsidian. The Olmecs developed writing, the calendar and the use of the zero. They had a strong artistic tradition, most notably the creation of massive sculptures of human heads.

San Lorenzo was abandoned around 900 BC, when La Venta became the main focus of Olmec culture. Their eventual demise around 400 BC was accompanied by a massive drop in population numbers. This is thought to have been caused by the impact of environmental change. For several centuries after the Olmecs the region consisted of relatively small states.

This list covers Olmec armies from 1150 to 400 BC.

TROOP NOTES

Before the rise of the Olmecs, weapons in the region were essentially hunting tools re-used for combat. The Olmecs improved the fire hardened sticks by adding stone and obsidian spearheads and blades. These allowed the weapons to be used to cut as well as to thrust. They also developed the use of clubs and maces. *Atlatls* were employed by the Olmecs, but there is no real evidence of them being used in a military context. The great majority of troops went without shields or armour.

Battle groups with Heavy Weapon capability are those with a high proportion of men armed with heavy clubs and maces.

OLMEC STARTER ARMY		
Commander-in-Chief	1	Field Commander
Sub-commanders	2	2 x Troop Commander
Nobles	2 BGs	Each comprising 8 bases of nobles: Superior, Unprotected, Drilled Medium Foot – Light Spear, Swordsmen
Nobles	2 BGs	Each comprising 8 bases of nobles: Superior, Unprotected, Drilled Medium Foot – Heavy Weapon
Commoners	2 BGs	Each comprising 10 bases of commoners: Average, Unprotected, Undrilled Medium Foot – Light Spear, Swordsmen
Commoners	1 BG	10 bases of commoners: Average, Unprotected, Undrilled Medium Foot – Heavy Weapon
Slingers	2 BGs	Each comprising 6 bases of slingers: Average, Unprotected, Undrilled Light Foot – Sling
Atlatl skirmishers	1 BG	8 bases of *atlatl* skirmishers: Average, Unprotected, Undrilled Light Foot – Javelins, Light Spear
Camp	1	Unfortified camp
Total	10 BGs	Camp, 82 foot bases, 3 commanders

BUILDING A CUSTOMISED LIST USING OUR ARMY POINTS

Choose an army based on the maxima and minima in the list below. The following special instructions apply to this army:

• Commanders should be depicted as nobles.

OLMEC

Territory Types: Agricultural, Developed, Tropical

C-in-C	Inspired Commander/Field Commander/Troop Commander			80/50/35	1	
Sub-commanders	Field Commander			50	0-2	
	Troop Commander			35	0-3	

Troop name	Troop Type				Capabilities		Points per base	Bases per BG	Total bases
	Type	Armour	Quality	Training	Shooting	Close Combat			
Core Troops									
Nobles	Medium Foot	Unprotected	Superior	Drilled	-	Light Spear, Swordsmen	7	6-8	12-36
	Medium Foot	Unprotected	Superior	Drilled	-	Heavy Weapon	8	6-8	0-18
Commoners	Medium Foot	Unprotected	Average	Undrilled	-	Light Spear, Swordsmen	5	6-10	20-120
	Medium Foot	Unprotected	Average	Undrilled	-	Heavy Weapon	6	6-10	6-24
Optional Troops									
Atlatl skirmishers	Light Foot	Unprotected	Average	Undrilled	Javelins	Light Spear	4	6-8	0-24
			Poor				2		
Slingers	Light Foot	Unprotected	Average	Undrilled	Sling	-	4		
			Poor				2		

TEOTIHUACAN

This list covers the armies of Teotihuacan from its emergence in 100 AD to its fall around 750.

The city-state of Teotihuacan formed the first major empire in the central valley of Mexico, just north-east of where Mexico City now stands. The empire dominated the local cities and its impact was felt from the arid north of Mexico down to the Mayan states in the steamy jungles of the Yucatán peninsula. The city came to prominence on the back of the obsidian trade – at its height there were over 400 obsidian workshops within Teotihuacan. The city was one of the largest in the world in its prime with perhaps 200,000 inhabitants. The colossal structures of the Pyramid of the Sun, Avenue of the Dead and Pyramid of the Moon are impressive even today.

Economic success led to expanding influence. In the 3rd century the Tula region came under Teotihuacan control. Expansion to the east increased influence over the state of Cholula, and developing trade routes out to the Gulf coast, the

Puebla valley and the North East. Eventually their influence spread as far as Kaminaljuyu, on the site of modern Guatemala City.

The fall of Teotihuacan is one of the mysteries of the ancient world. The most plausible theory is that the stresses caused by maintaining the empire with only foot transport led to a central collapse.

TROOP NOTES

The highest status warriors belonged to military societies based on animal themes: Jaguar, Eagle and Coyote. Members of these societies would wear feather-covered suits over their armour on the battlefield, each depicting the patron animal of their society.

The standard defensive equipment was a helmet and a smallish parrying shield with feather fringes. The shield was held from a strap at the top, and was flexible enough to be rolled up when not needed. From 450 AD quilted cotton armour was introduced. The armour was

5–7.5cm (2–3 inches) thick, in two varieties – one covering torso and limbs and the other torso and upper legs. However, this was costly as the cotton had to be imported – carried on foot – and it was a lot of work to quilt the armour. Hence it is less likely that the part-time commoners would have it, but we give the option of Protected in case a substantial proportion did.

Teotihuacan added the massed use of *atlatls* to the thrusting spear.

TEOTIHUACAN STARTER ARMY (FROM 450 AD)		
Commander-in-Chief	1	Field Commander
Sub-commanders	2	2 x Troop Commander
Military societies	4 BGs	Each comprising 8 bases of military societies: Superior, Protected, Drilled Medium Foot – Javelins, Light Spear, Swordsmen
Commoners	3 BGs	Each comprising 8 bases of commoners: Average, Unprotected, Undrilled Medium Foot – Javelins, Light Spear
Slingers	3 BGs	Each comprising 6 bases of slingers: Average, Unprotected, Undrilled Light Foot – Sling
Atlatl skirmishers	1 BG	6 bases of *atlatl* skirmishers: Average, Unprotected, Undrilled Light Foot – Javelins, Light Spear
Camp	1	Unfortified camp
Total	11 BGs	Camp, 80 foot bases, 3 commanders

BUILDING A CUSTOMISED LIST USING OUR ARMY POINTS

Choose an army based on the maxima and minima in the list below. The following special instructions apply to this army:

- Commanders should be depicted as Military Societies.

TEOTIHUACAN									
Territory Types: Agricultural, Developed, Hilly									
C-in-C	Inspired Commander/Field Commander/Troop Commander						80/50/35	1	
Sub-commanders	Field Commander						50	0-2	
	Troop Commander						35	0-3	
Troop name	Troop Type				Capabilities		Points per base	Bases per BG	Total bases
	Type	Armour	Quality	Training	Shooting	Close Combat			
Core Troops									
Military Societies	Only before 450	Medium Foot	Unprotected	Superior	Drilled	Javelins	Light Spear, Swordsmen	7	6-8	16-48
	Only from 450	Medium Foot	Protected	Superior	Drilled	Javelins	Light Spear, Swordsmen	9	6-8	
Commoners	Any date	Medium Foot	Unprotected	Average	Undrilled	Javelins	Light Spear	4	6-10	24-170
	Only from 450	Medium Foot	Protected	Average	Undrilled	Javelins	Light Spear	5	6-10	
Optional Troops									
Atlatl skirmishers	Light Foot	Unprotected	Average	Undrilled	Javelins	Light Spear	4	6-8	0-12
			Poor				2		
Slingers	Light Foot	Unprotected	Average	Undrilled	Sling	-	4	6-8	0-24
			Poor				2		

WEST MEXICAN

This list covers the armies of the states to the west of the central valley of Mexico and the Pacific coast from 100 to 900 AD. The most important sites were Ixtlan del Rio, Huitzilapa, Teuchitlan, Ameca and El Openo in the modern states of Nayarit, Jalisco, Colima, and Michoacán. These little-known cultures buried their dead in deep "shaft tombs" and much of what we know of them comes from ceramic figurines.

Unusually for Mesoamerica these cultures built circular cities around the circular equivalent of a step pyramid.

The western reaches of Mexico remained independent of the large central states. However, they suffered a marked decline around 900 AD, possibly related to pressure from the peoples who would later form the Tarascan empire to the east.

TROOP NOTES

Archaeological evidence shows extensive use of clubs, spears and slings.

In this period troops had protection for the torso from armour shaped like a barrel which may have been leather or perhaps stiffened fabric. This was augmented by wickerwork helmets. Cotton armour was not widely used until after the end date of this list.

Battle groups with Heavy Weapon capability are those with a high proportion of men armed with heavy bladed clubs.

WEST MEXICAN STARTER ARMY		
Commander-in-Chief	1	Field Commander
Sub-commanders	2	2 x Troop Commander
Nobles	1 BG	6 bases of nobles: Superior, Protected, Drilled Medium Foot – Heavy Weapon
Nobles	2 BGs	Each comprising 6 bases of nobles: Superior, Protected, Drilled Medium Foot – Light Spear, Swordsmen
Commoners	2 BGs	Each comprising 8 bases of commoners: Average, Unprotected, Undrilled Medium Foot – Heavy Weapon
Commoners	3 BGs	Each comprising 8 bases of commoners: Average, Protected, Undrilled Medium Foot – Light Spear, Swordsmen
Slingers	3 BGs	Each comprising 6 bases of slingers: Average, Unprotected, Undrilled Light Foot – Sling
Camp	1	Unfortified camp
Total	11 BGs	Camp, 76 foot bases, 3 commanders

BUILDING A CUSTOMISED LIST USING OUR ARMY POINTS

Choose an army based on the maxima and minima in the list below. The following special instructions apply to this army:

- Commanders should be depicted as nobles.
- West Mexican allied commanders' contingents must conform to the West Mexican allies list below, but the troops in the contingent are deducted from the minima and maxima in the main list.

WEST MEXICAN

Territory Types: Agricultural, Developed, Hilly

C-in-C	Inspired Commander/Field Commander/Troop Commander			80/50/35		1	
Sub-commanders	Field Commander/Troop Commander			50/35		0-2	
West Mexican allied commanders	Field Commander/Troop Commander			40/25		0-3	

Troop name	Troop Type				Capabilities		Points per base	Bases per BG	Total bases
	Type	Armour	Quality	Training	Shooting	Close Combat			
Core Troops									
Nobles	Medium Foot	Protected	Superior	Drilled	-	Light Spear, Swordsmen	9	6-8	8-24
	Medium Foot	Protected	Superior	Drilled	-	Heavy Weapon	10	6-8	0-8	8-24
Commoners	Medium Foot	Protected	Average	Undrilled	-	Light Spear, Swordsmen	6	6-10	24-128
	Medium Foot	Unprotected	Average	Undrilled	-	Light Spear, Swordsmen	5	6-10	0-96	24-128
	Medium Foot	Protected	Average	Undrilled	-	Heavy Weapon	7	6-10	0-96
	Medium Foot	Unprotected	Average	Undrilled	-	Heavy Weapon	6	6-10	
Optional Troops									
Slingers	Light Foot	Unprotected	Average	Undrilled	Sling	-	4	6-8	0-32
			Poor				2		

WEST MEXICAN ALLIES

Allied commander	Field Commander/Troop Commander					40/25		1	
Troop name	Troop Type				Capabilities		Points per base	Bases per BG	Total bases
	Type	Armour	Quality	Training	Shooting	Close Combat			
Nobles	Medium Foot	Protected	Superior	Drilled	-	Light Spear, Swordsmen	9	6-8	0-8
	Medium Foot	Protected	Superior	Drilled	-	Heavy Weapon	10	4-6	0-6	4-8
Commoners	Medium Foot	Protected	Average	Undrilled	-	Light Spear, Swordsmen	6	6-10	8-32
	Medium Foot	Unprotected	Average	Undrilled	-	Light Spear, Swordsmen	5	6-10	0-24
	Medium Foot	Protected	Average	Undrilled	-	Heavy Weapon	7	6-10	0-24	8-32
	Medium Foot	Unprotected	Average	Undrilled	-	Heavy Weapon	6	6-10	
Slingers	Light Foot	Unprotected	Average	Undrilled	Sling	-	4	6-8	0-8
			Poor				2		

ZAPOTEC OR MIXTEC

The three-lobed valley of Oaxaca, co-located with the modern Mexican state of that name, was a highly fertile region surrounded by mountains. At the junction of the three lobes, the Zapotec city of Monte Alban was built and fortified on a hilltop site around 500 BC and came to dominate the whole valley in later centuries. Expansion to the north eventually brought the Zapotecs,

Mixtec oracular priest, queen and slinger, by Angus McBride. Taken from Men-at-Arms 239: Aztec, Mixtec and Zapotec Armies.

around 400 AD, into contact with Teotihuacan, a state which was more powerful militarily and economically. The Zapotecs were forced to regroup into the Oaxaca valley itself. Monte Alban subsequently declined and Jalieza emerged as the most powerful of several small states in the valley.

Around 900 AD the Mixtecs invaded the Oaxaca valley. The petty Zapotec states were in no condition to repel them. The resulting Mixtec states were unified into an empire by King Eight Deer Jaguar Claw (1011–1063). Centred on the city of Tilantongo in the high mountains of the Mixteca Alta to the north-west of the Oaxaca valley, Eight Deer's empire included the valley itself and all the Mixtec peoples as far as Tututepec on the Pacific coast. Eight Deer's empire rapidly broke apart after his death, and the Mixtecs and Zapotecs went back to loose alliances of petty states.

Early Zapotec armies were relatively small and mainly comprised of nobles. However, contact with the Teotihuacan state increased the role of commoners in the army, resulting in larger armies.

Zapotec Archer

This list covers the armies of the Zapotec and Mixtec cultures from 400 AD to 1500 AD.

TROOP NOTES

The relatively isolated situation of the Oaxaca valley resulted in a conservative approach to military matters. Zapotec weaponry was a thrusting spear together with stone-headed clubs. Small round shields were used, and *atlatls* and slings provided missile fire. The military societies of the nobles used elaborate costumes depicting eagles and jaguars.

The Mixtecs continued the Jaguar and Eagle societies and their weapons systems were similar to the Zapotecs.

Pressure from the Chichimecs to the north introduced the bow in the 13th century and the Aztec broadsword was introduced later.

In the late 15th and early 16th century, the Mixtecs still used a distinctively shaped sword with a short obsidian blade and long handle, the whole weapon being about 1.2 metres (4 feet) long. This was another development from earlier Toltec sword-clubs. An earlier depiction of Mixtec weapons shows sword-clubs with a curved end, with an obsidian blade on the convex side only.

ZAPOTEC OR MIXTEC STARTER ARMY (BEFORE 1200 AD)		
Commander-in-Chief	1	Field Commander
Sub-commanders	2	2 x Troop Commander
Military societies	3 BGs	Each comprising 8 bases of military societies: Superior, Protected, Undrilled Medium Foot – Javelins, Light Spear, Swordsmen
Military societies	1 BG	8 bases of military societies: Superior, Protected, Undrilled Medium Foot – Heavy Weapon
Commoners	3 BGs	Each comprising 8 bases of warriors: Average, Protected, Undrilled Medium Foot – Javelins, Light Spear, Swordsmen
Slingers	2 BGs	Each comprising 6 bases of slingers: Average, Unprotected, Undrilled Light Foot – Sling
Atlatl skirmishers	1 BGs	Each comprising 6 bases of *atlatl* skirmishers: Average, Unprotected, Undrilled Light Foot – Javelins, Light Spear
Camp	1	Unfortified camp
Total	10 BGs	Camp, 74 foot bases, 3 commanders

Zapotec priest, warlord and drummer, by Angus McBride. Taken from Men-at-Arms 239: Aztec, Mixtec *and Zapotec Armies.*

BUILDING A CUSTOMISED LIST USING OUR ARMY POINTS

Choose an army based on the maxima and minima in the list below. The following special instructions apply to this army:

- Commanders should be depicted as Military societies.

- Eight Deer must be an Inspired Commander.
- Mixtec or Zapotec allied commanders' contingents must conform to the Mixtec or Zapotec allies list below, but the troops in the contingent are deducted from the minima and maxima in the main list.

ZAPOTEC OR MIXTEC

Territory Types: Agricultural, Developed, Hilly

C-in-C		Inspired Commander/Field Commander/Troop Commander				80/50/35		1	
Sub-commanders	Only Mixtecs under Eight Deer from 1011 to 1063	Field Commander/ Troop Commander				50/35		0-3	
	Others	Field Commander/Troop Commander				50/35		0-2	
Mixtec or Zapotec allied commanders		Field Commander/Troop Commander				40/25		0-2	
Troop name		**Troop Type**				**Capabilities**		**Points per base**	**Bases per BG**	**Total bases**
		Type	Armour	Quality	Training	Shooting	Close Combat			
Core Troops										
Military societies		Medium Foot	Protected	Superior	Undrilled	Javelins	Light Spear, Swordsmen	8	6-8	8-24
		Medium Foot	Protected	Superior	Undrilled	-	Heavy Weapon	9	6-8	0-8
Commoners		Medium Foot	Protected	Average	Undrilled	Javelins	Light Spear, Swordsmen	6	6-10	24-120
Slingers		Light Foot	Unprotected	Average	Undrilled	Sling	-	4	6-8	6-24
				Poor				2		
Atlatl skirmishers		Light Foot	Unprotected	Average	Undrilled	Javelins	Light Spear	4	6-8	6-18
				Poor				2		
Archers	Only from 1200	Medium Foot	Protected	Average	Undrilled	Bow	-	6	6-8	6-12
			Unprotected					5		
		Light Foot	Unprotected	Average	Undrilled	Bow	-	5	6-8	
				Poor				3		

ZAPOTEC OR MIXTEC ALLIES

Allied commander		Field Commander/Troop Commander				40/25		1	
Troop name		**Troop Type**				**Capabilities**		**Points per base**	**Bases per BG**	**Total bases**
		Type	Armour	Quality	Training	Shooting	Close Combat			
Military societies		Medium Foot	Protected	Superior	Undrilled	Javelins	Light Spear, Swordsmen	8	6-8	0-8 / 4-8
		Medium Foot	Protected	Superior	Undrilled	-	Heavy Weapon	9	4-6	0-6
Commoners		Medium Foot	Protected	Average	Undrilled	Javelins	Light Spear, Swordsmen	6	6-10	8-32
Slingers		Light Foot	Unprotected	Average	Undrilled	Sling	-	4	6-8	0-8
				Poor				2		
Atlatl skirmishers		Light Foot	Unprotected	Average	Undrilled	Javelins	Light Spear	4	4-6	0-6 / 4-18
				Poor				2		
Archers	Only from 1200	Medium Foot	Protected	Average	Undrilled	Bow	-	6	4	0-4
			Unprotected					5		
		Light Foot	Unprotected	Average	Undrilled	Bow	-	5	4	
				Poor				3		

Mixtec standard bearer, priest and warlord, by Angus McBride. Taken from Men-at-Arms 239: Aztec, Mixtec and Zapotec Armies.

TOLTEC

The Toltecs were the successors to Teotihuacan in central Mexico. The largest centre was that of Tula or Tollan that grew to dominate the region. This culture generated the legend of Quetzalcoatl – a godlike mighty lord – who departed over the sea to the east. Much later, Cortez was to play on this legend to wrong-foot the Aztecs. Later cultures looked back on Tollan times as a golden age.

Toltec culture featured human sacrifice, a rack for holding the skulls of those sacrificed being prominent at Tula. The Toltecs were very much a trading empire, with influence reaching as far as the modern south-western USA and Guatemala. This was backed up by an efficient army.

The region suffered a worsening climate toward the end of the Toltec reign, with a pronounced drying of the region resulting in famine. The Toltecs were finally brought down by Chichimec nomads from the arid north of Mexico, whose access to bow and arrow technology was something new. There is evidence that Tula fell in 1179 AD, probably following

economic decline owing to Chichimec disruption.

This list covers Toltec armies from 900 to 1179 AD.

TROOP NOTES

In terms of military developments the main Toltec contribution was to take an existing short club with obsidian blades and lengthen it into something that was part sword and part club. Shields evolved to become circular. *Atlatls* were heavily used.

The main way of war seemed to be an intense bombardment of *atlatl* javelins/darts following which the warriors would advance with shield and sword/club to close quarters.

There is evidence of warriors in Coyote and Jaguar costumes which were presumably military societies of some type. There is also evidence of sling use.

While there is no evidence that the Toltecs adopted the bow, it is highly probable that they used Chichimec tribes as auxiliaries on occasion.

TOLTEC STARTER ARMY		
Commander-in-Chief	1	Field Commander
Sub-commanders	2	2 x Troop Commander
Military societies	2 BGs	Each comprising 6 bases of military societies: Superior, Protected, Undrilled Medium Foot – Javelins, Light Spear, Swordsmen
Military societies	1 BG	6 bases of military societies: Superior, Protected, Undrilled Medium Foot – Heavy Weapon
Warriors	4 BGs	Each comprising 8 bases of warriors: Average, Protected, Undrilled Medium Foot – Javelins, Light Spear, Swordsmen
Atlatl skirmishers	2 BGs	Each comprising 6 bases of *atlatl* skirmishers: Average, Unprotected, Undrilled Light Foot – Javelins, Light Spear
Slingers	2 BGs	Each comprising 6 bases of slingers: Average, Unprotected, Undrilled Light Foot – Sling
Chichimec auxiliaries	1 BG	8 bases of Chichimec auxiliaries: Average, Unprotected, Undrilled Light Foot – Bow
Camp	1	Unfortified camp
Total	12 BGs	Camp, 82 foot bases, 3 commanders

BUILDING A CUSTOMISED LIST USING OUR ARMY POINTS

Choose an army based on the maxima and minima in the list below. The following special instructions apply to this army:

- Commanders should be depicted as military societies.

TOLTEC									
Territory Types: Agricultural, Developed, Hilly									
C-in-C	Inspired Commander/Field Commander/Troop Commander						80/50/35	1	
Sub-commanders	Field Commander						50	0-2	
	Troop Commander						35	0-3	
Troop name	Troop Type				Capabilities		Points per base	Bases per BG	Total bases
	Type	Armour	Quality	Training	Shooting	Close Combat			
Core Troops									
Coyote or Jaguar military societies	Medium Foot	Protected	Superior	Undrilled	Javelins	Light Spear, Swordsmen	8	6-8	0-16 · 6-18
	Medium Foot	Protected	Superior	Undrilled	-	Heavy Weapon	9	6-8	0-8
Warriors	Medium Foot	Protected	Average	Undrilled	Javelins	Light Spear, Swordsmen	6	6-10	24-120
Atlatl skirmishers	Light Foot	Unprotected	Average	Undrilled	Javelins	Light Spear	4	6-8	6-36
Slingers	Light Foot	Unprotected	Average	Undrilled	Sling	-	4	6-8	6-24
Optional Troops									
Chichimec auxiliaries	Light Foot	Unprotected	Average	Undrilled	Bow	-	5	6-8	0-12

CHINANTEC

The Chinantecs lived in the mountainous north of Oaxaca. Their towns included Atlatlauca, Chinantla, Oxitlan, Tepetotutla, Tlacoatzintepec, Tuxtepec and Ucila. They were conquered by the Aztecs in the late 15th century, but parts of the area had regained their independence before the arrival of the Spanish.

This list covers Chinantec armies from 1300 to 1500 AD.

TROOP NOTES

The main weapons were long spears, bows and swords.

The Spanish were very impressed by the Chinantec spears, which were about 4.9 metres (16 feet) in length, with 1.7 metres (5.5 feet) of obsidian blade at the tip. Although the blades were presumably designed to slash, their length, which prompted the Spanish to describe them as pikes, suggests a classification as Medium Foot Offensive Spearmen. The spearmen fought naked, apart from a breech-clout of maguey fibre, but carried long, quilted fabric shields. These covered the whole body when fighting, but could be rolled up when not in use.

Chinantec nobles fought with bow rather than spear, and wore quilted cotton body armour.

CHINANTEC STARTER ARMY		
Commander-in-Chief	1	Field Commander
Sub-commanders	2	2 x Troop Commander
Nobles	2 BGs	Each comprising 6 bases of nobles: Superior, Protected, Undrilled Medium Foot – Bow, Swordsmen
Spearmen	5 BGs	Each comprising 8 bases of spearmen: Average, Protected, Undrilled Medium Foot – Offensive Spearmen
Archers	2 BGs	Each comprising 6 bases of archers: Average, Unprotected, Undrilled Light Foot – Bow
Slingers	1 BG	8 bases of slingers: Average, Unprotected, Undrilled Light Foot - Sling
Camp	1	Unfortified camp
Total	10 BGs	Camp, 72 foot bases, 3 commanders

BUILDING A CUSTOMISED LIST USING OUR ARMY POINTS

Choose an army based on the maxima and minima in the list below. The following special instructions apply to this army:

- Commanders should be depicted as nobles.
- Chinantec allied commanders' contingents must conform to the Chinantec allies list below, but the troops in the contingent are deducted from the minima and maxima in the main list.

CHINANTEC									
Territory Types: Mountains, Agricultural									
C-in-C	Inspired Commander/Field Commander/Troop Commander						80/50/35	1	
Sub-commanders	Field Commander/Troop Commander						50/35	0-2	
Chinantec allied commanders	Field Commander/Troop Commander						40/25	0-3	
Troop name	Troop Type				Capabilities		Points per base	Bases per BG	Total bases
	Type	Armour	Quality	Training	Shooting	Close Combat			
Core Troops									
Nobles	Medium Foot	Protected	Superior	Undrilled	Bow	Swordsmen	9	6-8	6-12
Spearmen	Medium Foot	Protected	Average	Undrilled	-	Offensive Spearmen	7	8-10	24-132
Archers	Light Foot	Unprotected	Average	Undrilled	Bow	-	5	6-8	0-24
Slingers	Light Foot	Unprotected	Average	Undrilled	Slingers	-	4	6-8	0-12 / 0-24
			Poor				2		

CHINANTEC ALLIES									
Allied commander	Field Commander/Troop Commander						40/25	1	
Troop name	Troop Type				Capabilities		Points per base	Bases per BG	Total bases
	Type	Armour	Quality	Training	Shooting	Close Combat			
Nobles	Medium Foot	Protected	Superior	Undrilled	Bow	Swordsmen	9	4-6	4-6
Spearmen	Medium Foot	Protected	Average	Undrilled	-	Offensive Spearmen	7	8-10	8-32
Archers	Light Foot	Unprotected	Average	Undrilled	Bow	-	5	6-8	0-8

Huaxtec patrol ambushed by Aztec troops, by Adam Hook. Taken from Warrior 32: Aztec Warrior AD 1325–1521.

AZTEC

By 1300 AD there had been a slow recovery from a post classical dark age in Central America. Political organisation was by city-state throughout most of the region, although the arid north of modern-day Mexico was dominated by wandering Chichimec tribes. One of those tribes, calling themselves the Mexica (whom we know, owing to a misunderstanding by the Spanish, as the Aztecs) had been allowed to settle on a swampy island in the brackish waters of Lake Mexico as subjects of the Tepanec empire (which was ruled from Azcapotzalco on the western shore). There they founded the island city of Tenochtitlan in 1325. Tlacopan was one of the subject cities of the Tepanec empire on the western shore close to Tenochtitlan. On the eastern shore were a number of cities of Acolhua ethnicity, including Tetzcoco.

Over time, Tepanec rule spread to include Tetzcoco and a number of other cities on the eastern shore of the lake.

Under the rule of the splendidly-named

Warrior Priest

21

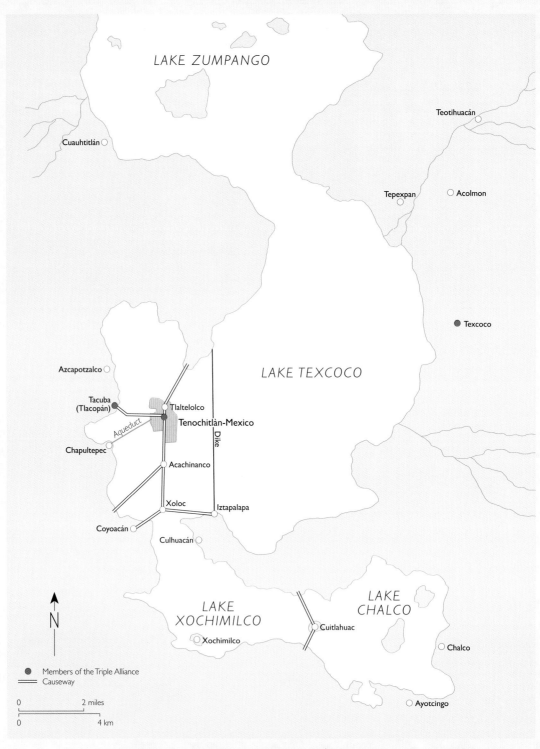

LAKE ZUMPANGO

Teotihuacán

Cuauhtitlán

Tepexpan   Acolmon

Texcoco

Azcapotzalco   LAKE TEXCOCO

Tacuba
(Tlacopán)   Tlaltelolco

Aqueduct   Tenochitlàn-Mexico

Chapultepec   Dike

Acachinanco

Xoloc   Iztapalapa

Coyoacán

Culhuacán

LAKE   LAKE
XOCHIMILCO   CHALCO

Cuitlahuac

Xochimilco   Chalco

● Members of the Triple Alliance
═══ Causeway

Ayotcingo

0   2 miles

0   4 km

The Valley of Mexico. Taken from Essential Histories 60: The Spanish Invasion of Mexico 1519–1521.

Itzcohuatl "Obsidian Serpent" (1427–1440) the Aztecs, supported by Tlacopan and Tetzcoco, rose up and overthrew their Tepanec overlords. The Aztecs did not have the power to consolidate the shattered Tepanec empire on their own, so entered into a long-term Triple Alliance with Tlacopan and Tetzcoco, which they came to dominate. Itzcohuatl rewrote their history and redefined their religion, bringing the blood god Huitzilopochtli to prominence. The god needed to be fed with an increasing stream of human sacrifice. The acquisition of large numbers of prisoners for sacrifice came to be one of the main features of warfare. Warriors gained rank by brave deeds and taking captives.

In little over a century of almost constant politics and warfare, the Aztecs had built a mighty empire that dominated Central America and placed significant pressure on the other major powers of the region, the Tlaxcalans, Totonacs and Maya. They established a hegemony over their neighbours, who were required to provide food, shelter and troops for the Aztec army. Their subsequent overthrow by a combination of Tlaxcala and the Spanish conquistadors was all the more dramatic for taking place at the height of their power.

Logistics were a critical issue for all Central American armies. The lack of wheeled or animal transport meant that all the supplies for the armies had to be carried by hand. This meant that a third of the manpower of the army was devoted to porterage. Roads were rudimentary and narrow. With no carts, most roads were unpaved and could only be travelled two abreast. Consequently, the army would divide into divisions of 8,000 for strategic manoeuvre.

This list covers Aztec armies from 1375 to 1500 AD.

TROOP NOTES

The rise of the Aztecs coincided with a change of the weapons used in the region. The bow (*tlahuitolli*) gave a longer range than the sling or the spear thrower (*atlatl*) though these were still used. Obsidian-edged broadswords (*macuahuitl*) and cutting spears (*tepoztopilli*) replaced the earlier system of heavy clubbing weapons though these were still used to some degree.

Aztec shields were recorded by Spanish sources as strong, and were between 51–76cm (20–30 inches) in diameter, sometimes with a feather-decorated fringe below. Many of the warriors wore quilted cotton body armour under their decorative war suits. However, some at least chose to fight naked apart from their shields.

The *calpolli* or city ward was the standard means of organising and training the bulk of the army.

Promotion was based on captives taken (for subsequent sacrifice) and bravery in battle. Experienced warriors gained the right to clothing and shields covered in bright feather work and wore helmets of carved wood painted to represent eagles and jaguars. Eagle and Jaguar military societies were reserved for warriors who had taken at least four captives. Jaguar society warriors are more common than Eagle society warriors in pictorial sources, and Eagle warriors are frequently depicted as more senior commanders; so it seems that they held some sort of seniority over the Jaguars. Military society battle groups can be assumed to include a proportion of less experienced noble warriors.

Cuachic with macuahuitl

Warriors would reach the rank of *Otontin* with five captives, and *Cuachicqueh* with six. These senior warriors could either fight in their own units or stiffen the ranks of less experienced warriors.

Aztec Eagle warrior, Jaguar warrior and priest, by Angus McBride. Taken from Men-at-Arms 101: The Conquistadores.

AZTEC STARTER ARMY		
Commander-in-Chief	1	Field Commander
Sub-commanders	2	2 x Troop Commander
Cuachicqueh	1 BG	6 bases of Cuachicqueh: Elite, Protected, Drilled Medium Foot – Javelins, Impact Foot, Swordsmen
Otontin	1 BG	6 bases of Otontin: Superior, Protected, Drilled Medium Foot – Javelins, Impact Foot, Swordsmen
Military societies	2 BGs	Each comprising 6 bases of military societies: Superior, Protected, Drilled Medium Foot – Javelins, Impact Foot, Swordsmen
Calpolli foot	2 BGs	Each comprising 8 bases of Calpolli foot: Average, Protected, Drilled Medium Foot – Javelins, Impact Foot, Swordsmen
Slingers	1 BG	8 bases of slingers: Average, Unprotected, Drilled Light Foot - Sling
Slingers	1 BG	6 bases of slingers: Average, Unprotected, Drilled Light Foot - Sling
Archers	1 BG	8 bases of archers: Average, Unprotected, Undrilled Light Foot - Bow
Camp	1	Unfortified camp
Total	9 BGs	Camp, 62 foot bases, 3 commanders

BUILDING A CUSTOMISED LIST USING OUR ARMY POINTS

Choose an army based on the maxima and minima in the list below. The following special instructions apply to this army:

- Commanders should be depicted as military societies, though other figures can be mixed in.
- Triple Alliance troops from Tlacopan or Tetzcoco can be assumed to be amongst the troops comprising the main army, or can be used under allied commanders. In the latter case, each Triple Alliance allied commander's contingent must conform to the Triple Alliance allies

Triple Alliance Slinger

list below, but the troops in the contingent are deducted from the minima and maxima in the main list.

- Central American allies can be used under an allied commander as per normal. Alternatively, they can be incorporated in the main army, and count in line of command of C-in-C and sub-commanders. If this option is used an allied commander cannot be used for these troops (though a second allied contingent could have one), and the minima for both main list and Central American allies list apply.

Eagle Warrior

Aztec levy troops, by Angus McBride. Taken from Men-at-Arms 101: The Conquistadores.

AZTEC

Territory Types: Agricultural, Developed, Hilly

C-in-C	Inspired Commander/Field Commander/Troop Commander	80/50/35		1
Sub-commanders	Field Commander	50		0-2
	Troop Commander	35		0-3
Triple Alliance allied commanders	Only from 1427	Field Commander/Troop Commander	40/25	0-2

Troop name	Troop Type				Capabilities		Points per base	Bases per BG	Total bases
	Type	Armour	Quality	Training	Shooting	Close Combat			
Core Troops									
Cuachicqueh	Medium Foot	Protected	Elite	Drilled	Javelins	Impact Foot, Swordsmen	12	6-8	0-12
Military societies or Otontin	Medium Foot	Protected	Superior	Drilled	Javelins	Impact Foot, Swordsmen	10	6-8	8-36
Calpolli foot	Medium Foot	Protected	Average	Drilled	Javelins	Impact Foot, Swordsmen	8	6-10	16-84 (16-84)
	Medium Foot	Protected	Average	Undrilled	Javelins	Impact Foot, Swordsmen	7	6-10	0-24
Slingers	Light Foot	Unprotected	Average	Undrilled	Sling	-	4	6-8	0-24 (6-36)
Archers	Light Foot	Unprotected	Average	Undrilled	Bow	-	5	6-8	0-24
Optional Troops									
Archers	Medium Foot	Protected	Average	Undrilled	Bow	-	6	6-8	0-8
Pits, barricades, stone walls	Field Fortifications	-	-	-	-	-	3	-	0-8
Allies									
Central American Allies (up to 2 contingents) (Only from 1427)									

TRIPLE ALLIANCE ALLIES

Allied commander	Field Commander/Troop Commander						40/25		1
Troop name	Troop Type				Capabilities		Points per base	Bases per BG	Total bases
	Type	Armour	Quality	Training	Shooting	Close Combat			
Cuachicqueh	Medium Foot	Protected	Elite	Drilled	Javelins	Impact Foot, Swordsmen	12	4	0-4
Military societies or Otontin	Medium Foot	Protected	Superior	Drilled	Javelins	Impact Foot, Swordsmen	10	6-8	6-12
Calpolli foot	Medium Foot	Protected	Average	Drilled	Javelins	Impact Foot, Swordsmen	8	6-10	8-24 (8-24)
	Medium Foot	Protected	Average	Undrilled	Javelins	Impact Foot, Swordsmen	7	8	0-8
Slingers	Light Foot	Unprotected	Average	Undrilled	Sling	-	4	6-8	0-8 (0-12)
Archers	Light Foot	Unprotected	Average	Undrilled	Bow	-	5	6-8	0-8

CENTRAL AMERICAN ALLIES

Allied commander	Field Commander/Troop Commander						40/25		1
Troop name	Troop Type				Capabilities		Points per base	Bases per BG	Total bases
	Type	Armour	Quality	Training	Shooting	Close Combat			
Military Societies	Medium Foot	Protected	Superior	Drilled	Javelins	Impact Foot, Swordsmen	10	8	0-8
Calpolli foot	Medium Foot	Protected	Average	Drilled	Javelins	Impact Foot, Swordsmen	8	6-10	16-48
				Undrilled			7		
	Medium Foot	Protected	Poor	Drilled	Javelins	Impact Foot, Swordsmen	6	6-10	0-24
				Undrilled			5		
Slingers	Light Foot	Unprotected	Average	Undrilled	Sling	-	4	6-8	0-24 (6-24)
Archers	Light Foot	Unprotected	Average	Undrilled	Bow	-	5		0-24

Mexica cuachic warriors at the forefront of the Aztec battleline, by Adam Hook. Taken from Warrior 32: Aztec Warrior AD 1325–1521.

TARASCAN

The Tarascan empire was the most formidable opponent of the Aztecs, inflicting a heavy defeat on them and maintaining a balance of power thereafter. Its capital city of Tzintzuntzan was located on the shore of Lake Patzcuato, in the modern Mexican state of Michoacan. The geography was primarily mountainous. The people were mainly from the P'urhepecha ethnic group.

While the P'urhepecha had been long residents of the region, they were first unified by Tariacuri, who forged them into an empire and formed a dynasty. His descendents extended the empire to incorporate the regions around Lake Cuitzeo, the Tarascan sierra and the Balsas basin. Further

expansion to the north and west followed until the Pacific was reached. In the east, the Tarascans were on a collision course with the Aztecs. Conflicts between the two started in the 1470s and continued on and off until the Spanish conquest.

Tarascan Archers

The Tarascans adopted a largely defensive stance here, erecting fortifications and settling tribes on the frontier to defend it.

This list covers Tarascan armies from 1300 to 1500 AD.

TROOP NOTES

This area did not produce cotton, so the locally-produced armour was made out of the tough fibres of the maguey plant, though this was supplemented with imported cotton.

Tarascan nobles – the *Tiacham* or "Valiant Ones" – fought hand to hand with obsidian broadswords and clubs. The bulk of the army though was made up of commoners who fought as unarmoured archers.

The *Tiacham* would normally form up in the centre, flanked and supported by massed archers. Battle Groups with Heavy Weapon capability are those with a high proportion of men armed with two-handed clubs.

The Tarascans made more use of metal than others in the region, with some copper weapons being present.

TARASCAN STARTER ARMY		
Commander-in-Chief	1	Field Commander
Sub-commanders	2	2 x Troop Commander
Tiacham	3 BGs	Each comprising 6 bases of Tiacham: Superior, Protected, Undrilled Medium Foot – Impact Foot, Swordsmen
Tiacham	2 BGs	Each comprising 6 bases of Tiacham: Superior, Protected, Undrilled Medium Foot – Heavy Weapon
Archers	3 BGs	Each comprising 8 bases of archers: Average, Unprotected, Undrilled Medium Foot - Bow
Archers	3 BGs	Each comprising 6 bases of archers: Average, Unprotected, Undrilled Light Foot – Bow
Camp	1	Unfortified camp
Total	11 BGs	Camp, 72 foot bases, 3 commanders

BUILDING A CUSTOMISED LIST USING OUR ARMY POINTS

Choose an army based on the maxima and minima in the list below. The following special instructions apply to this army:

• Commanders should be depicted as *Tiacham*.

TARASCAN

Territory Types: Mountains, Hilly, Agricultural, Developed

C-in-C	Inspired Commander/Field Commander/Troop Commander					80/50/35		1	
Sub-commanders	Field Commander					50		0-2	
	Troop Commander					35		0-3	
Troop name	**Troop Type**				**Capabilities**		**Points per base**	**Bases per BG**	**Total bases**
	Type	Armour	Quality	Training	Shooting	Close Combat			
Core Troops									
Tiacham	Medium Foot	Protected	Superior	Undrilled	-	Impact Foot, Swordsmen	9	6-8	8-36 / 8-36
	Medium Foot	Protected	Superior	Undrilled	-	Heavy Weapon	9	6-8	0-12
Archers	Medium Foot	Unprotected	Average	Undrilled	Bow	-	5	6-8	24-160
			Poor				3		
Optional Troops									
Slingers	Light Foot	Unprotected	Average	Undrilled	Sling	-	4	6-8	0-12 / 0-36
Archers	Light Foot	Unprotected	Average	Undrilled	Bow	-	5	6-8	0-36

TLAXCALAN CONFEDERACY

The Tlaxcalan confederacy consisted of a number of *Nahuatl* speaking city-states, located in the modern Mexican state of Tlaxcala, who had formed a loose alliance due to pressure from their neighbours, notably the Aztecs. They inhabited the lands between the central valley of Mexico and the Gulf coast. While alliances shifted, the state of Tlaxcala was usually the prime mover. Tlaxcala itself was subdivided into four political entities – Ocotelolco, Quiahuiztlan, Tepeticpac and Tizatlan. The leaders of Tlaxcala were supplied from these four on a rotational basis.

The Tlaxcalan confederacy formed a bulwark against Aztec expansion eastwards and were their implacable enemies. Over several decades the two powers went to war with each other every year. Not all of these were all-out affairs. Many were of a form of ritualised, low intensity combat known as a Flower War, which put some pressure on the opposition, blooded the troops, and, critically, provided captives for sacrifice.

The Tlaxcalan confederacy initially put up a fierce resistance to the Spanish. However, old hatreds overcame them, and they decided that they would rather ally with the newcomers to destroy the Aztecs. In doing so, they earned a privileged position in post-conquest Mexico.

Tlaxcalan Inspired Commander

TROOP NOTES

The Tlaxcalan confederacy made more use of missile weapons, particularly bows, than their Aztec neighbours but otherwise used a very similar weapons system.

Tlaxcalan warriors, by Angus McBride. Taken from Men-at-Arms 239: Aztec, Mixtec and Zapotec Armies.

TLAXCALAN STARTER ARMY		
Commander-in-Chief	1	Field Commander
Sub-commanders	2	2 x Troop Commander
Military societies	3 BGs	Each comprising 6 bases of military societies: Superior, Protected, Drilled Medium Foot – Javelins, Impact Foot, Swordsmen
Calpolli foot	2 BGs	Each comprising 8 bases of Calpolli foot: Average, Protected, Undrilled Medium Foot – Javelins, Impact Foot, Swordsmen
Archers	2 BGs	Each comprising 8 bases of archers: Average, Protected, Undrilled Medium Foot – Bow
Archers	2 BGs	Each comprising 6 bases of archers: Average, Unprotected, Undrilled Light Foot – Bow
Slingers	1 BG	8 bases of slingers: Average, Unprotected, Drilled Light Foot – Sling
Camp	1	Unfortified camp
Total	10 BGs	Camp, 70 foot bases, 3 commanders

BUILDING A CUSTOMISED LIST USING OUR ARMY POINTS

Choose an army based on the maxima and minima in the list below. The following special instructions apply to this army:

- Commanders should be depicted as military societies.
- Tlaxcalan allied commanders' contingents must conform to the Tlaxcalan allies list below, but the troops in the contingent are deducted from the minima and maxima in the main list.

Tlaxcalan Field Commander

Tlaxcalan Troop Commander

TLAXCALAN CONFEDERACY

Territory Types: Agricultural, Developed, Hilly

C-in-C	Inspired Commander/Field Commander/Troop Commander					80/50/35	1	
Sub-commanders	Field Commander/Troop Commander					50/35	0-2	
Tlaxcalan allied commanders	Field Commander/Troop Commander					40/25	0-2	

Troop name	Troop Type				Capabilities		Points per base	Bases per BG	Total bases
	Type	Armour	Quality	Training	Shooting	Close Combat			
Core Troops									
Military Societies	Medium Foot	Protected	Superior	Drilled	Javelins	Impact Foot, Swordsmen	10	6-8	6-36
Calpolli foot	Medium Foot	Protected	Average	Drilled	Javelins	Impact Foot, Swordsmen	8	6-10	12-36
				Undrilled			7		
	Medium Foot	Protected	Poor	Drilled	Javelins	Impact Foot, Swordsmen	6	6-10	0-24
				Undrilled			5		
Archers	Medium Foot	Protected	Average	Undrilled	Bow	-	6	6-8	16-48
Optional Troops									
Slingers	Light Foot	Unprotected	Average	Undrilled	Sling	-	4	6-8	0-24
Archers	Light Foot	Unprotected	Average	Undrilled	Bow	-	5	6-8	0-36	0-36
Pits, barricades, stone walls	Field Fortifications	-	-	-	-	-	3	-	0-8
Allies									
Central American Allies (up to 2 contingents)									

TLAXCALAN ALLIES

Allied Commander	Field Commander/Troop Commander					40/25	1	

Troop name	Troop Type				Capabilities		Points per base	Bases per BG	Total bases
	Type	Armour	Quality	Training	Shooting	Close Combat			
Military Societies	Medium Foot	Protected	Superior	Drilled	Javelins	Impact Foot, Swordsmen	10	6-8	6-12
Calpolli foot	Medium Foot	Protected	Average	Drilled	Javelins	Impact Foot, Swordsmen	8	6-10	8-12
				Undrilled			7		
	Medium Foot	Protected	Poor	Drilled	Javelins	Impact Foot, Swordsmen	6	6-8	0-8
				Undrilled			5		
Archers	Medium Foot	Protected	Average	Undrilled	Bow	-	6	6-8	6-16
Slingers	Light Foot	Unprotected	Average	Undrilled	Sling	-	4	6-8	0-8
Archers	Light Foot	Unprotected	Average	Undrilled	Bow	-	5	6-8	0-12	0-12

Huexotzingan warrior, Tlaxcalan general and priest of Cholula or Coixtlahuaca, by Angus McBride.
Taken from Men-at-Arms 239: Aztec, Mixtec and Zapotec Armies.

MAYAN

The Mayan city-states were a constant presence from the jungles of Mexico's Yucatán peninsula to those of Guatemala. They were influenced and occasionally conquered by the other major states of Central America but absorbed the incomers into the Mayan culture.

The history of Mayan civilization is conventionally divided into three periods – Pre-Classical, Classical and Post-Classical. The Pre-Classical period lasted from c.1800 BC until c.200 AD.

The Classical period, during which urbanisation, with the construction of large stepped pyramids and palaces, reached its peak, lasted from then until 900. In this period, southern Mayan city-states included Tik'al, Palenque (B'aakal), Copán (Xukpi), Calakmul, Caracol (possibly Oxhuitza), Naranjo (Wak Kab'nal), and Yaxchilan (Pa' Chan), amongst others. Northern centres in the early Classical period included Oxkintok, Chunchucmil and Uxmal.

At the end of the Classical period, the southern Mayan centres collapsed, possibly as a result of a prolonged drought – although numerous other explanations have been advanced. The northern centres continued to flourish, however, in the Post-Classical period, from 900 AD. Important city-states in the earlier part of this period included Chichen Itza, Uxmal, Edzná, and Coba. In 1221 the Maya revolted against the rulers of Chichen Itza, and subsequently built the new city of Mayapan, which, under the kings of the Cocom family, dominated all of Yucatán until it was destroyed in 1450 following a revolt by the powerful Xiu family. Thereafter, Yucatán fell apart into competing city-states until the Spanish conquest. The last Mayan states (in northern modern Guatemala) remained independent until 1697.

This list covers Mayan armies from 600 BC until 1450 AD.

TROOP NOTES

The city-state of Tikal achieved dominance in the 4th century by the use of Teotihuacan troops. The state of Chichen Itza introduced Toltec military methods in the Post-Classical age.

The high rainfall in the Mayan lands made agriculture possible more or less throughout the year. Hence, in Pre-Classical times, commoners were generally unavailable for military service. Logistics (poor roads and lack of transportable foodstuffs) restricted the numbers that could travel. Armies tended to be small and composed mostly of nobles. Large battles were the exception. This all changed in the Classical period, when the state of Tikal, under its splendidly-named ruler Smoking Frog, introduced Teotihuacan troops, *atlatl* missile fire and the use of non-noble troops into the army. The neighbouring states were swept away, being outnumbered and outmatched.

Battle groups with Heavy Weapon capability are those with a high proportion of men armed with heavy clubs.

Around 1300 AD the Maya began to adopt the Aztec inspired obsidian broadsword which allowed shock charges to be more effective.

Mayan Warrior

Mayan Archer

MAYAN STARTER ARMY (POST-CLASSICAL FROM 1300 AD)		
Commander-in-Chief	1	Field Commander
Sub-commanders	2	2 x Troop Commander
Holcan professional troops	2 BGs	Each comprising 6 bases of Holcan professional troops: Superior, Protected, Drilled Medium Foot – Javelins, Impact Foot, Swordsmen
Nobles and military societies	2 BGs	Each comprising 6 bases of military societies: Superior, Protected, Undrilled Medium Foot – Javelins, Impact Foot, Swordsmen
Commoners	4 BGs	Each comprising 8 bases of commoners: Average, Protected, Undrilled Medium Foot – Bow, Light Spear
Skirmishing archers	2 BGs	Each comprising 6 bases of archers: Average, Unprotected, Undrilled Light Foot – Bow
Camp	1	Unfortified camp
Total	10 BGs	Camp, 68 foot bases, 3 commanders

BUILDING A CUSTOMISED LIST USING OUR ARMY POINTS

Choose an army based on the maxima and minima in the list below. The following special instructions apply to this army:

- Commanders should be depicted as nobles, military societies or Teotihuacan troops (Classical Tikal only).

- Armies must be either Pre-Classical, Classical or Post-Classical.
- Mayan allied commanders' contingents must conform to the Mayan allies list below, but the troops in the contingent are deducted from the minima and maxima in the main list.

Field Commander

Mayan Nobles

MAYAN

MAYAN									
Territory Types: Agricultural, Developed, Tropical, Hilly									
C-in-C		Inspired Commander/Field Commander/Troop Commander					80/50/35		1
Sub-commanders	Pre- and Post-Classical	Field Commander/Troop Commander					50/35		0-2
	Classical								0-3
Mayan allied commanders		Field Commanders/Troop Commander					40/25		0-3

Troop name		Troop Type				Capabilities		Points per base	Bases per BG	Total bases
		Type	Armour	Quality	Training	Shooting	Close Combat			
Core Troops										
Nobles and military societies	Only Pre-Classical	Medium Foot	Unprotected	Superior	Undrilled	-	Light Spear, Swordsmen	6	6-8	24-176	32-176
		Medium Foot	Unprotected	Superior	Undrilled	-	Heavy Weapon	7	6-8	0-32
	Only Classical	Medium Foot	Protected	Superior	Undrilled	-	Light Spear, Swordsmen	8	6-8	24-112	24-112
		Medium Foot	Protected	Superior	Undrilled	-	Heavy Weapon	9	6-8	0-24
	Only Post-Classical from 900 to 1299	Medium Foot	Protected	Superior	Undrilled	Javelins	Light Spear, Swordsmen	8	6-8	12-48
	Only Post-Classical from 1300	Medium Foot	Protected	Superior	Undrilled	Javelins	Impact Foot, Swordsmen	9	6-8	12-48
Commoners	Only Pre-Classical or Classical	Medium Foot	Unprotected	Average	Undrilled	-	Light Spear	5	6-10	0-20	0-20
		Medium Foot	Unprotected	Poor	Undrilled	-	Light Spear	3	8-10	
		Medium Foot	Unprotected	Average	Undrilled	-	Heavy Weapon	6	6-8	0-8
				Poor				4		
	Only Post-Classical	Medium Foot	Protected	Average	Undrilled	Bow	Light Spear	6	6-8	24-100
		Medium Foot	Protected	Poor	Undrilled	Bow	Light Spear	4	8	
Optional Troops										
Teotihuacan troops in Tikal armies	Only Classical from 350 to 500	Medium Foot	Protected	Superior	Drilled	Javelins	Light Spear, Swordsmen	9	6-8	0-24
Toltec troops in Chichen Itza armies	Only Post-Classical from 900 to 1100	Medium Foot	Protected	Superior	Undrilled	Javelins	Light Spear, Swordsmen	8	6-8	0-18
Holcan professional troops	Only Post-Classical from 1300	Medium Foot	Protected	Superior	Drilled	Javelins	Impact Foot, Swordsmen	10	6-8	0-18
Slingers		Light Foot	Unprotected	Average	Undrilled	Sling	-	4	6-8	Classical 0-36, Post-Classical 0-12
Skirmishing archers	Only Post-Classical	Light Foot	Unprotected	Average	Undrilled	Bow	-	5	6-8	0-24
Atlatl skirmishers		Light Foot	Unprotected	Average	Undrilled	Javelins	Light Spear	4	6-8	Classical 0-36, Post-Classical 0-12
Field Fortifications	Only Pre-Classical	Field Fortifications						3		0-20

Mayan general, warrior and peasant levy, by Angus McBride. Taken from Men-at-Arms 101:
The Conquistadores.

MAYAN ALLIES

Allied commander		Field Commanders/Troop Commander					40/25		1	
Troop name		Troop Type				Capabilities	Points per base	Bases per BG	Total bases	
		Type	Armour	Quality	Training	Shooting	Close Combat			
Nobles and military societies	Only Pre-Classical	Medium Foot	Unprotected	Superior	Undrilled	-	Light Spear, Swordsmen	6	6-8	8-48	8-48
		Medium Foot	Unprotected	Superior	Undrilled	-	Heavy Weapon	7	6-8	0-12	
	Only Classical	Medium Foot	Protected	Superior	Undrilled	-	Light Spear, Swordsmen	8	6-8	8-32	8-32
		Medium Foot	Protected	Superior	Undrilled	-	Heavy Weapon	9	6-8	0-8	
	Only Post-Classical from 900 to 1299	Medium Foot	Protected	Superior	Undrilled	Javelins	Light Spear, Swordsmen	8	6-8	6-16	
	Only Post-Classical from 1300	Medium Foot	Protected	Superior	Undrilled	Javelins	Impact Foot, Swordsmen	9	6-8	6-16	
Commoners	Only Pre-Classical or Classical	Medium Foot	Unprotected	Average	Undrilled	-	Light Spear	4	6	0-6	
				Poor				2			
	Only Post-Classical	Medium Foot	Protected	Average	Undrilled	Bow	Light Spear	6	6-8	8-32	
				Poor				4			
Holcan professional troops	Only Post-Classical from 1300	Medium Foot	Protected	Superior	Drilled	Javelins	Impact Foot, Swordsmen	10	4-6	0-6	
Slingers		Light Foot	Unprotected	Average	Undrilled	Sling	-	4	6-8	Classical 0-12, Post-Classical 0-6	
Skirmishing archers	Only Post-Classical	Light Foot	Unprotected	Average	Undrilled	Bow	-	5	6-8	0-8	
Atlatl skirmishers		Light Foot	Unprotected	Average	Undrilled	Javelins	Light Spear	4	6-8	Classical 0-12, Post-Classical 0-6	

MOCHICA

This list covers Mochica, or Moche, armies from 100 to 700 AD.

The Mochica or Moche culture dominated the northern coast of Peru, from the Pacific Ocean to the Andes. They were masters of ceramics and gold work and constructed massive mud brick pyramids, the largest being the Huaca del Sol on the Rio Moche.

Their political structure was dictated by the terrain. Eight fertile river valleys separated by desert gave each valley a good degree of independence. Irrigation was a critical part of the structure of society. Capture and sacrifice of the enemy was a significant part of warfare, with enemy heads being prominently displayed.

The Mochica were seriously affected by climatic disaster in the 6th century – 30 years of intense rain and flooding were followed by 30 years of drought – and never really recovered. They were succeeded by the Wari and Chimu empires.

TROOP NOTES

While slings and atlatls were in wide usage, the decisive hand to hand weapons were clubs up to 1.5 metres (5 feet) long. Square shields were used, about 40cm (16 inches) wide, and seem to have been used mostly to parry. Some of the warriors, perhaps the nobles, wore padded armour.

MOCHICA STARTER ARMY

Commander-in-Chief	1	Field Commander
Sub-commanders	2	2 x Troop Commander
Nobles	4 BGs	Each comprising 6 bases of nobles: Superior, Protected, Undrilled Medium Foot – Heavy Weapon
Commoners	3 BGs	Each comprising 10 bases of commoners: Average, Unprotected, Undrilled Medium Foot – Heavy Weapon
Atlatl skirmishers	3 BGs	Each comprising 6 bases of *atlatl* skirmishers: Average, Unprotected, Undrilled Light Foot – Javelins, Light Spear
Slingers	1 BG	6 bases of slingers: Poor, Unprotected, Undrilled Light Foot – Sling
Camp	1	Unfortified camp
Total	11 BGs	Camp, 78 foot bases, 3 commanders

BUILDING A CUSTOMISED LIST USING OUR ARMY POINTS

Choose an army based on the maxima and minima in the list below. The following special instructions apply to this army:

- Commanders should be depicted as nobles.
- Mochica allied commanders' contingents must conform to the Mochica allies list below, but the troops in the contingent are deducted from the minima and maxima in the main list.

MOCHICA

Territory Types: Agricultural, Desert

Troop name							Points per base	Bases per BG	Total bases
C-in-C	Inspired Commander/Field Commander/Troop Commander						80/50/35		1
Sub-commanders	Field Commander/ Troop Commander						50/35		0-2
Mochica allied commanders	Field Commander/ Troop Commander						40/25		0-3
	Troop Type				Capabilities		Points per base	Bases per BG	Total bases
	Type	Armour	Quality	Training	Shooting	Close Combat			
Core Troops									
Nobles	Medium Foot	Protected	Superior	Undrilled	-	Heavy Weapon	9	6-8	12-36
Commoners	Medium Foot	Unprotected	Average	Undrilled	-	Heavy Weapon	6	8-10	20-130
Optional Troops									
Atlatl skirmishers	Light Foot	Unprotected	Average	Undrilled	Javelins	Light Spear	4	6-8	0-24
			Poor				2		
Slingers	Light Foot	Unprotected	Average	Undrilled	Sling	-	4	6-8	
			Poor				2		

Mochica warrior, by Peter Dennis.

MOCHICA ALLIES

Allied commander	Field Commander/ Troop Commander						40/25	1	
Troop name	Troop Type				Capabilities		Points per base	Bases per BG	Total bases
	Type	Armour	Quality	Training	Shooting	Close Combat			
Nobles	Medium Foot	Protected	Superior	Undrilled	-	Heavy weapon	9	6-8	6-12
Commoners	Medium Foot	Unprotected	Average	Undrilled	-	Heavy Weapon	6	8-10	8-32
Atlatl skirmishers	Light Foot	Unprotected	Average	Undrilled	Javelins	Light Spear	4	4-6	0-8
			Poor				2		
Slingers	Light Foot	Unprotected	Average	Undrilled	Sling	-	4	4-6	
			Poor				2		

CHANCA

The Chanca lived in the Ayacucho area of Peru. Originally subjects of the Wari empire, they gained their independence around 1000. When the Wari empire collapsed around 1200, the Chanca expanded to fill the void.

The Chancas came into conflict with the rapidly growing Inca state and caught them unawares by launching a sudden thrust at the Inca capital in 1438. The resulting Battle of Cuzco saw the Incas block the Chancas frontally with pits and stakes and then hit their flanks. The Incas, now keenly aware of the threat that the Chancas posed, launched a campaign against them and broke their power. Shortly thereafter the Chanca became part of the Inca empire.

This list covers Chanca armies from 1000 to 1450 AD.

TROOP NOTES

Chanca warriors wore quilted cotton armour, for at least a proportion, and carried a small square shield. The primary weapon of the Chanca was the long spear, typically 3–4 metres (10–13 feet) in length. The mace was also used as a sidearm.

Chanca armies seem to have been quite light on skirmishers – having difficulty dealing with Inca slingers, for example.

CHANCA STARTER ARMY

Commander-in-Chief	1	Field Commander
Sub-commanders	2	2 x Troop Commander
Veteran spearmen	2 BGs	Each comprising 6 bases of veteran spearmen: Superior, Protected, Undrilled Medium Foot – Offensive Spearmen
Spearmen	6 BGs	Each comprising 8 bases of spearmen: Average, Protected, Undrilled Medium Foot – Offensive Spearmen
Skirmishers	1 BG	6 bases of skirmishers: Average, Unprotected, Undrilled Light Foot – Sling
Skirmishers	1 BG	6 bases of skirmishers: Poor, Unprotected, Undrilled Light Foot - Sling
Camp	1	Unfortified camp
Total	10 BGs	Camp, 72 foot bases, 3 commanders

BUILDING A CUSTOMISED LIST USING OUR ARMY POINTS

Choose an army based on the maxima and minima in the list below. The following special instructions apply to this army:

- Commanders should be depicted as veteran spearmen

CHANCA

Territory Types: Agricultural, Hilly, Developed

Troop name	Troop Type				Capabilities		Points per base	Bases per BG	Total bases
C-in-C	Inspired Commander/Field Commander/Troop Commander						80/50/35	1	
Sub-commanders	Field Commander						50	0-2	
	Troop Commander						35	0-3	
	Type	Armour	Quality	Training	Shooting	Close Combat			
Core Troops									
Spearmen	Medium Foot	Protected	Average	Undrilled	-	Offensive Spearmen	7	8-10	32-130
		Unprotected					6		
Optional Troops									
Veteran spearmen	Medium Foot	Protected	Superior	Undrilled	-	Offensive Spearmen	9	6-8	0-24
Skirmishers	Light Foot	Unprotected	Average	Undrilled	Sling	-	4	6-8	0-12
			Poor				2		

CHANCA ALLIES

Troop name	Troop Type				Capabilities		Points per base	Bases per BG	Total bases
Allied commander	Field Commander/ Troop Commander						40/25	1	
	Type	Armour	Quality	Training	Shooting	Close Combat			
Veteran spearmen	Medium Foot	Protected	Superior	Undrilled	-	Offensive Spearmen	9	6-8	0-8
Spearmen	Medium Foot	Protected	Average	Undrilled	-	Offensive Spearmen	7	8-10	8-32
		Unprotected					6		
Skirmishers	Light Foot	Unprotected	Average	Undrilled	Sling	-	4	4	0-4
			Poor				2		

CHIMU

The Chimu, or Kingdom of Chimor, ruled the northern coastal strip of Peru from c.850 to c.1470 AD. At its greatest extent, the Chimu empire extended along the coast for 1,000 km (600 miles). The Chimu were the cultural inheritors of the earlier Mochica culture.

The Chimu capital of Chan Chan was in the Moche valley, near modern Trujillo. In a harsh desert climate cut through by rivers, the Chimu developed extensive irrigation techniques including underground reservoirs.

Chimor was the last kingdom that stood any chance of halting Inca expansion. However, its emperor, Minchancaman, was defeated by Túpac Inca c.1470.

TROOP NOTES

Chimu troops wore quilted armour for the torso, carried shields and were armed with heavy maces and clubs. Support troops used *atlatl*-launched javelins, mace and shield.

CHIMU STARTER ARMY

Commander-in-Chief	1	Field Commander
Sub-commanders	2	2 x Troop Commander
Veteran warriors	2 BGs	Each comprising 8 bases of veteran warriors: Superior, Protected, Undrilled Medium Foot – Heavy Weapon
Warriors	1 BG	10 bases of warriors: Average, Protected, Undrilled Medium Foot – Heavy Weapon
Warriors	3 BGs	Each comprising 8 bases of warriors: Average, Protected, Undrilled Medium Foot – Heavy Weapon
Atlatl skirmishers	4 BGs	Each comprising 6 bases of atlatl skirmishers: Average, Unprotected, Undrilled Light Foot – Javelins, Light Spear
Camp	1	Unfortified camp
Total	10 BGs	Camp, 74 foot bases, 3 commanders

BUILDING A CUSTOMISED LIST USING OUR ARMY POINTS

Choose an army based on the maxima and minima in the list below. The following special instructions apply to this army:

- Commanders should be depicted as veteran warriors

CHIMU

Territory Types: Agricultural, Desert

C-in-C	Inspired Commander/Field Commander/Troop Commander				80/50/35		1	
Sub-commanders	Field Commander				50		0-2	
	Troop Commander				35		0-3	

Troop name	Troop Type				Capabilities		Points per base	Bases per BG	Total bases
	Type	Armour	Quality	Training	Shooting	Close Combat			
Core Troops									
Warriors	Medium Foot	Protected	Average	Undrilled	-	Heavy Weapon	7	8-10	32-120
Optional Troops									
Veteran warriors	Medium Foot	Protected	Superior	Undrilled	-	Heavy Weapon	9	6-8	0-24
Atlatl skirmishers	Light Foot	Unprotected	Average	Undrilled	Javelins	Light Spear	4	6-8	0-24
			Poor				2		

CHIMU ALLIES

Allied commander	Field Commander/ Troop Commander				40/25		1	

Troop name	Troop Type				Capabilities		Points per base	Bases per BG	Total bases
	Type	Armour	Quality	Training	Shooting	Close Combat			
Veteran warriors	Medium Foot	Protected	Superior	Undrilled	-	Heavy Weapon	9	6-8	0-8
Warriors	Medium Foot	Protected	Average	Undrilled	-	Heavy Weapon	7	8-10	8-40
Atlatl skirmishers	Light Foot	Unprotected	Average	Undrilled	Javelins	Light Spear	4	6-8	0-8
			Poor				2		

HATUN-COLLA

This list covers the armies of Hatun-Colla ("the great kingdom of Colla") from 1400 to 1460 AD.

Hatun-Colla was a state centred on the Western edge of Lake Titicaca, near modern Juliaca on the Peru–Bolivian border. Under its young king, Ruquicapana, it conquered the neighbouring states of Canas and Chiribaya and allied with La Paz. It came to grief against the Luparca, allies of the Incas. Ruquicapana was killed and Luparca and the Incas divided Hatun-Colla between them.

TROOP NOTES

Hatun-Colla nobles used spear and swords made out of the wood of the Chonta tree, with quilted armour for the torso and round shields. The common warriors had spears, small hand maces and no armour.

Canas allies used mace and bolas, which we categorise as equivalent to a Light Spear at impact and had quilted armour. Chiribaya troops used wicker shields.

HATUN-COLLA STARTER ARMY		
Commander-in-Chief	1	Field Commander
Sub-commanders	2	2 x Troop Commander
Nobles	6 BGs	Each comprising 6 bases of nobles: Superior, Protected, Undrilled Medium Foot – Light Spear, Swordsmen
Colla spearmen	3 BGs	Each comprising 8 bases of Colla spearmen: Average, Unprotected, Undrilled Medium Foot – Light Spear
Skirmishers	4 BGs	Each comprising 6 bases of skirmishers: Average, Unprotected, Undrilled Light Foot – Sling
Camp	1	Unfortified camp
Total	13 BGs	Camp, 84 foot bases, 3 commanders

BUILDING A CUSTOMISED LIST USING OUR ARMY POINTS

Choose an army based on the maxima and minima in the list below. The following special instructions apply to this army:

- Commanders should be depicted as nobles.

HATUN-COLLA

Territory Types: Agricultural, Developed, Hilly

C-in-C		Inspired Commander/Field Commander/Troop Commander					80/50/35	1	
Sub-commanders		Field Commander					50	0-2	
		Troop Commander					35	0-3	
Troop name		Troop Type				Capabilities	Points per base	Bases per BG	Total bases
		Type	Armour	Quality	Training	Shooting	Close Combat		
Core Troops									
Nobles		Medium Foot	Protected	Superior	Undrilled	-	Light Spear, Swordsmen	8	6-8	16-48
Colla spearmen		Medium Foot	Unprotected	Average	Undrilled	-	Light Spear	4	8-10	24-170
Optional Troops									
Skirmishers		Light Foot	Unprotected	Average	Undrilled	Sling	-	4	6-8	0-24
				Poor				2		
La Paz auxiliaries	Only from 1455	Medium Foot	Unprotected	Average	Undrilled	-	Light Spear	4	8-10	0-50
Chiribaya levies	Only from 1460	Medium Foot	Protected	Average	Undrilled	-	Light Spear	5	8-10	0-50
				Poor				3		
Allies									
Canas allies (Only from 1455)									

CANAS ALLIES

Allied commander		Field Commander/Troop Commander					40/25	1	
Troop name		Troop Type				Capabilities	Points per base	Bases per BG	Total bases
		Type	Armour	Quality	Training	Shooting	Close Combat		
Warriors		Medium Foot	Protected	Average	Undrilled	-	Light Spear, Swordsmen	6	8-10	8-40
Skirmishers		Light Foot	Unprotected	Average	Undrilled	Sling	-	4	6-8	0-8

CAÑARI

This list covers armies of the Cañari kingdom from 1400 to 1460 AD, when they were absorbed by the Incas.

The Cañari kingdom was a loose confederation of tribes in south central Ecuador, Their two major cities were Tumipampa and Cuispampa. They were defeated by Túpac Inca and incorporated into the Inca empire. Thereafter, Cañari spearmen formed part of the *Sapa Inca*'s personal guard, being regarded as more trustworthy than the Inca nobility.

The Cañari came to a bad end. In the Inca civil war between the two sons of Huayna Cápac,

Huascar and Atahualpa, they were on Huascar's losing side. The victorious Atahualpa raised Tumipampa to the ground and massacred its inhabitants.

TROOP NOTES

The Cañari weapon was the long spear – typically 3–4 metres (10–13 feet) in length. Some of the troops wielding this wore wicker armour on the torso. South American forces with such spears did not stand up particularly well to Spanish mounted in open terrain, so we class them as Medium Foot Offensive Spearmen.

CAÑARI STARTER ARMY

Commander-in-Chief	1	Field Commander
Sub-commanders	2	2 x Troop Commander
Elite spearmen	2 BGs	Each comprising 8 bases of spearmen: Superior, Protected, Undrilled Medium Foot – Offensive Spearmen
Spearmen	5 BGs	Each comprising 8 bases of spearmen: Average, Protected, Undrilled Medium Foot – Offensive Spearmen
Atlatl skirmishers	1 BG	6 bases of atlatl skirmishers: Average, Unprotected, Undrilled Light Foot – Javelins, Light Spear
Slingers	2 BGs	Each comprising 8 bases of slingers: Poor, Unprotected, Undrilled Light Foot – Sling
Camp	1	Unfortified camp
Total	10 BGs	Camp, 78 foot bases, 3 commanders

BUILDING A CUSTOMISED LIST USING OUR ARMY POINTS

Choose an army based on the maxima and minima in the list below. The following special instructions apply to this army:

- Commanders should be depicted as elite spearmen.
- Cañari allied commanders' contingents must conform to the Cañari allies list below, but the troops in the contingent are deducted from the minima and maxima in the main list.

CAÑARI

Territory Types: Agricultural, Desert

C-in-C	Inspired Commander/Field Commander/Troop Commander						80/50/35		1
Sub-commanders	Field Commander/ Troop Commander						50/35		0-2
Cañari allied commanders	Field Commander/ Troop Commander						40/25		0-3

Troop name	Troop Type				Capabilities		Points per base	Bases per BG	Total bases
	Type	Armour	Quality	Training	Shooting	Close Combat			
Core Troops									
Elite Spearmen	Medium Foot	Protected	Superior	Undrilled	-	Offensive Spearmen	9	6-8	12-36
Spearmen	Medium Foot	Protected	Average	Undrilled	-	Offensive Spearmen	7	8-10	20-120
		Unprotected					6		
Optional Troops									
Atlatl skirmishers	Light Foot	Unprotected	Average	Undrilled	Javelins	Light Spear	4	6-8	0-24
			Poor				2		
Slingers	Light Foot	Unprotected	Average	Undrilled	Sling	-	4	6-8	
			Poor				2		

Cañari warrior, by Peter Dennis.

CAÑARI ALLIES

Allied commander		Field Commander / Troop Commander					40/25	1	
Troop name	Troop Type				Capabilities		Points per base	Bases per BG	Total bases
	Type	Armour	Quality	Training	Shooting	Close Combat			
Elite Spearmen	Medium Foot	Protected	Superior	Undrilled	-	Offensive Spearmen	9	6-8	6-12
Spearmen	Medium Foot	Protected	Average	Undrilled	-	Offensive Spearmen	7	8-10	8-32
		Unprotected					6		
Atlatl skirmishers	Light Foot	Unprotected	Average	Undrilled	Javelins	Light Spear	4	4-6	0-8
			Poor				2		
Slingers	Light Foot	Unprotected	Average	Undrilled	Sling	-	4	4-6	
			Poor				2		

INCA

From 1438 AD, Pachahutec Inca Yupanqui, the ninth *Sapa Inca* (king) of the small Quechua city-state of Cuzco (in south-eastern Peru) conquered most of southern Peru. Cuzco was rebuilt as the capital of the new empire. From 1463, his son Túpac Inca began conquests to the north, continuing after his accession to the throne on the death of his father in 1471, and extending the empire to include north-western Peru and most of Equador. His most important conquest was the coastal kingdom of Chimor. The Inca empire reached its maximum extent under his son Huayna Cápac (1493–1527), who added much territory to the south, extending the empire as far as the south of Chile, and made additional conquests in the north.

By the end of his reign the Inca empire controlled almost the full length of the Andes, including much of modern Peru, Ecuador and Chile, with parts of Bolivia, Argentina and Colombia. Its population numbered up to 10 million. It was highly organised, with an extensive road system joining all of its main provinces. Agriculture was intensive, a system of hillside terracing making maximum use of the available land, and the roads allowed for efficient food distribution. The empire was quite capable of raising armies of over 100,000 men without over-straining its resources.

At its height the empire encompassed hundreds of different tribes, each with its own culture, divided into four main linguistic groups – Quechua, Chimu (on the coast), Aymara (in the south) and Uru (in the north). The official language was Quechua.

Between 1532 and 1539 the Inca empire, divided against itself by a dynastic civil war, was conquered by an astonishingly small number of Spanish conquistadors. A remnant state in the mountains of Vilcabamba (straddling the Peruvian–Bolivian border) lasted until 1572.

This list covers Inca armies from 1438 until 1500.

TROOP NOTES

Veterans (*huaminca*) were the Inca regiments raised from the capital, Cuzco. They received formal military training from adolescence. The vast majority of troops, however, comprised conscripted militia from throughout the empire, with equipment supplied by the state. However, weaponry varied according to previous tribal custom – for example, the Conchi used slings, darts and bolas, while the Chuncho and Anti used bows. Each nationality within the Inca army was required by law to wear distinctive tribal insignia, which sometimes involved the colours and patterns of stripes in their *uncu* (the standard Inca sleeveless, shapeless shirt), but mainly head-gear or hair style. Infringement was punishable by 100 lashes.

Some Inca guardsmen were armed with a halberd (*yauri*). Following the conquest of Cañar

Sapa Inca on Litter

Inca generals, by Angus McBride. Taken from Men-at-Arms 101: The Conquistadores.

by Túpac Inca, Cañari spearmen were recruited as royal guardsmen – the loyalty of the Inca nobility being increasingly suspect. The royal guard then also included Anti or Chuncho archers.

Some full-time troops were maintained as frontier garrisons – from the 1490s these were mainly recruited from the Cañari. We classify the earlier units the same as the militia.

The usual Inca shield was a small square of wood with a long fabric apron below. In addition to this, which we do not treat as sufficient to convey Protected status on its own, close combat troops also wore cotton-padded cloth body armour (of the same shape as the normal civilian uncu) and quilted cotton and wood or plaited cane helmets.

Spear and halberd heads were copper or bronze. Spear shafts were often fringed with feathers. Most troops also carried a one-handed mace with a star-shaped stone or metal head – we treat this as giving Swordsmen capability when used by close combat troops. All ranks of society used the sling, the *Sapa Inca* using slingshot of gold! However, roles were differentiated in battle, so we do not give the close combat troops sling capability. The standard plan was to soften up the enemy with massed slingers, archers, dart throwers and bolas men prior to the hand-to-hand clash of the close combat specialists. The enemy was often engaged by only one third of the army, while the remainder either stood in reserve or attempted to outflank the enemy.

Chanca and Cañari were armed with longer spears than those used by the Incas. Chimu were armed with heavy maces and clubs. Charca were armed with 1.2 metre (4 feet) long 2-handed black chonta-wood swords, 10cm (4 inches) wide at the tip.

INCA STARTER ARMY		
Commander-in-Chief	1	Field Commander
Sub-commanders	2	2 x Troop Commander
Inca noble guardsmen	1 BG	6 bases of Inca noble guardsmen: Superior, Protected, Drilled Medium Foot – Heavy Weapon
Veteran spearmen	2 BGs	Each comprising 6 bases of veteran spearmen: Superior, Protected, Drilled Medium Foot – Light Spear, Swordsmen
Militia spearmen	3 BGs	Each comprising 6 bases of militia spearmen: Average, Protected, Drilled Medium Foot – Light Spear, Swordsmen
Militia slingers	6 BGs	Each comprising 6 bases of militia slingers: Average, Unprotected, Drilled Light Foot – Sling
Chuncho archers	1 BG	6 bases of Chuncho archers: Average, Unprotected, Undrilled Light Foot – Bow
Conchi dart and bolas skirmishers	1 BG	6 bases of Conchi dart and bolas skirmishers: Poor, Unprotected, Undrilled Light Foot – Javelins, Light Spear
Camp	1	Unfortified camp
Total	14 BGs	Camp, 84 foot bases, 3 commanders

The expansion of the Inca empire. Taken from Fortress 47: Fortifications of the Incas: 1200–1531.

BUILDING A CUSTOMISED LIST USING OUR ARMY POINTS

Choose an army based on the maxima and minima in the list below. The following special instructions apply to this army:

- The C-in-C should be depicted carried on a litter if the *Sapa Inca*, otherwise as guardsmen. Sub-commanders should be depicted as guardsmen or veterans.
- The number of battle groups of Poor militia slingers cannot exceed the number of battle groups of Poor militia spearmen.

- Chanca or Chimu troops from the main list cannot be used with allies of the same nationality.

Inca Spearmen

Machu Picchu, by Adam Hook. Taken from Fortress 47: Fortifications of the Incas: 1200–1531.

INCA

Territory Types: Mountains, Hilly, Developed										
C-in-C	Inspired Commander/Field Commander/Troop Commander							80/50/35	1	
Sub-commanders	Field Commander							50	0-2	
	Troop Commander							35	0-3	
Troop name	Troop Type				Capabilities		Points per base	Bases per BG	Total bases	
	Type	Armour	Quality	Training	Shooting	Close Combat				
Core Troops										
Veteran spearmen	Medium Foot	Protected	Superior	Drilled	-	Light Spear, Swordsmen	9	6-8	6-18	
Militia spearmen	Medium Foot	Protected	Average	Drilled	-	Light Spear, Swordsmen	7	6-8	12-56	
			Poor				5			
Militia slingers	Light Foot	Unprotected	Average	Drilled	Sling	-	4	6-8	16-80	
			Poor				2			
Optional Troops										
Inca noble guardsmen	Medium Foot	Protected	Superior	Drilled	-	Heavy Weapon	10	4-6	0-6	0-10
Cañari guardsmen (Only from 1490)	Medium Foot	Protected	Superior	Drilled	-	Offensive Spearmen	10	4-6 or 2/3 of 6-9	0-6	
Anti or Chuncho guardsmen (Only from 1490)	Light Foot	Unprotected	Superior	Drilled	Bow	-	6	1/3 of 6-9 or 4	0-4	
	Medium Foot	Unprotected	Superior	Drilled	Bow	Swordsmen	8	4		
Anti, Chuncho or other forest tribe archers	Light Foot	Unprotected	Average	Undrilled	Bow	-	5	6-8	0-16	
			Poor				3			
	Medium Foot	Unprotected	Average	Undrilled	Bow	Swordsmen	6	6-8		
			Poor				4			
Conchi, Colla or similar skirmishers with darts and/or bolas	Light Foot	Unprotected	Average	Undrilled	Javelins	Light Spear	4	6-8	0-8	
			Poor				2			
Chanca spearmen	Medium Foot	Protected	Average	Undrilled	-	Offensive Spearmen	7	6-8	0-12	0-18
			Poor				5			
Chimu warriors	Medium Foot	Protected	Average	Undrilled	-	Heavy Weapon	7	6-8	0-12	
			Poor				5			
Charca warriors	Medium Foot	Unprotected	Average	Undrilled	-	Heavy Weapon	6	6-8	0-8	
			Poor				4			
Chiribaya or similar spearmen	Medium Foot	Protected	Average	Undrilled	-	Light Spear	5	6-8	0-12	
			Poor				3			
La Paz or similar spearmen	Medium Foot	Unprotected	Average	Undrilled	-	Light Spear	4	6-8	0-12	
			Poor				2			
Cañari spearmen (Only from 1490)	Medium Foot	Protected	Average	Drilled	-	Offensive Spearmen	8	6-8	0-12	
			Average	Undrilled			7			
			Poor	Undrilled			5			
Pits and chonta wood stakes	Field Fortifications						3		0-16	
Allies										
Chanca allies										
Chimu allies										

Chinchaysuyu warrior, Quechua slinger and Chimor warrior, by Angus McBride.
Taken from *Men-at-Arms 101: The Conquistadores.*

MAPUCHE OR ARAUCANIAN

This list covers the Northern and Southern Mapuche armies, the Spanish name for the Southerners being Araucanian. The origin of the Mapuche is unclear, though DNA evidence suggests a Polynesian link. While they existed from 500 AD, the great majority of information we have comes from their interactions with the Incas, then the Spanish (outside our period). Hence this list is for their armies from 1461, the first significant encounter with the Incas, to 1500.

The Mapuche inhabited what is today northern Chile. They successfully resisted the Incas, being the only South American people to hold their own against Túpac Inca, whom they fought to a bloody standstill at the Battle of the Maule. Indeed the strength of the Southern Mapuche was such that they gave the Spanish a very hard time later in the 16th and 17th centuries.

TROOP NOTES

The Mapuche were each trained from the early age in the use of a single weapon. The Spanish felt this was intended to make them masters in the use of that weapon, rather than semi-competent with several. The exception seems to have been that those armed with bow were also armed with a heavy luma-wood club (*lonco quillquill*), between 2 and 3 metres (6 to nearly 10 feet) in length. It was curved at the end somewhat in the same manner as a hockey stick.

The Northern Mapuche used archers and also troops with short spears.

The Southern Mapuche were more formidable. In addition to archers they used very long spears – up to 25 palmas long according to the Spanish (3–4 metres or 10–13 feet). These were "packed together in a squadron like Germans" – presumably referring to *Landsknechts*. However, as they retired to difficult going to fight the Spanish cavalry, rather than stand against them in open ground, we classify them as Medium Foot Offensive Spearmen.

Alonzo de Ercilla, writing in the mid-16th century, describes them as wearing "strong double corselets, and something like a skirt, armbands, throat guard and caps of hard leather". The leather was sealskin (perhaps also llama skin), worn until it hardened. Some of the spearmen, at least, carried medium-sized shields.

SOUTHERN MAPUCHE STARTER ARMY		
Commander-in-Chief	1	Field Commander
Sub-commanders	2	2 x Troop Commander
Archers	4 BGs	Each comprising 6 bases of archers: Average, Protected, Undrilled Medium Foot – Bow*, Heavy Weapon
Spearmen	4 BGs	Each comprising 8 bases of spearmen: Average, Protected, Undrilled Medium Foot – Offensive Spearmen
Skirmishers	2 BGs	Each comprising 6 bases of skirmishers: Average, Unprotected, Undrilled Light Foot – Bow
Camp	1	Unfortified camp
Total	10 BGs	Camp, 68 foot bases, 3 commanders

Mapuche warrior, by Peter Dennis.

BUILDING A CUSTOMISED LIST USING OUR ARMY POINTS

Choose an army based on the maxima and minima in the list below. The following special instructions apply to this army:

- Commanders should be depicted as warriors
- An army must be either Southern or Northern Mapuche, and cannot include troops from the other region.

MAPUCHE OR ARAUCANIAN

Territory Types: Agricultural, Woodland, Hilly

C-in-C		Inspired Commander/Field Commander/Troop Commander					80/50/35		1	
Sub-commanders		Field Commander					50		0-2	
		Troop Commander					35		0-3	
Troop name		Troop Type				Capabilities		Points per base	Bases per BG	Total bases
		Type	Armour	Quality	Training	Shooting	Close Combat			
Core Troops										
Archers	Only Northern	Medium Foot	Protected	Average	Undrilled	Bow*	Heavy Weapon	8	6-8	12-84
			Unprotected					7		
	Only Southern	Medium Foot	Protected	Average	Undrilled	Bow*	Heavy Weapon	8	6-8	12-72
			Unprotected					7		
Spearmen	Only Northern	Medium Foot	Protected	Average	Undrilled	-	Light Spear	5	8-10	20-84
			Unprotected					4		
	Only Southern	Medium Foot	Protected	Average	Undrilled	-	Offensive Spearmen	7	8-10	20-72
			Unprotected					6		
Optional Troops										
Skirmishers		Light Foot	Unprotected	Average	Undrilled	Bow	-	5	6-8	0-24 / 0-24
		Light Foot	Unprotected	Poor	Undrilled	Bow	-	3	6-8	0-8

AMAZONIAN FOREST TRIBES

The cannibalistic and primitive Amazonian forest tribes such as the Anti, Muzu, Pausas and Chuncho fought the expanding Inca empire and became auxiliaries in its armies.

This list covers the Amazonian forest tribes from 1350 to 1500 AD.

TROOP NOTES

The defining weapon of the Amazonian tribes was the chonta-wood bow, which was long, typically 2 metres (6 feet) or more, but had relatively poor penetrating power even against textile armour. Secondary weapons were usually clubs and sometimes axes. Some use was made of spear-throwers – when mixed in with a majority of bowmen we treat the overall effect as Bow.

Most tribes used smallish shields of wood, leather or basket-work, and fought naked apart from a penis-sheath or breech-clout. Face and body paint was usual. Some tribes wore head-dresses of brightly coloured feathers. Chieftains might cover their bodies all over with stuck-on feathers.

Amazonian Warriors

AMAZONIAN FOREST TRIBES STARTER ARMY

Commander-in-Chief	1	Field Commander
Sub-commanders	2	2 x Troop Commander
Veteran warriors	2 BGs	Each comprising 8 bases of veteran warriors: Superior, Unprotected, Undrilled, Medium Foot – Bow, Swordsmen
Warriors	5 BGs	Each comprising 8 bases of warriors: Average, Unprotected, Undrilled Medium Foot – Bow, Swordsmen
Warriors	3 BGs	Each comprising 6 bases of warriors: Average, Unprotected, Undrilled Light Foot – Bow
Subject tribe foot	2 BGs	Each comprising 6 bases of subject tribe foot: Poor, Unprotected, Undrilled Light Foot – Bow
Camp	1	Unfortified camp
Total	12 BGs	Camp, 86 foot bases, 3 commanders

BUILDING A CUSTOMISED LIST USING OUR ARMY POINTS

Choose an army based on the maxima and minima in the list below. The following special instructions apply to this army:

- Commanders should be depicted as veteran warriors.
- Amazonian allied commanders' contingents must conform to the Amazonian Forest Tribes allies list below, but the troops in the contingent are deducted from the minima and maxima in the main list.

AMAZONIAN FOREST TRIBES

Territory Types: Tropical

Troop name	Troop Type				Capabilities		Points per base	Bases per BG	Total bases
C-in-C	Inspired Commander/Field Commander/Troop Commander						80/50/35		1
Sub-commanders	Field Commander/Troop Commander						50/35		0-2
Amazonian allied commanders	Field Commander/Troop Commander						40/25		0-3
	Type	Armour	Quality	Training	Shooting	Close Combat			
Core Troops									
Warriors	Medium Foot	Unprotected	Average	Undrilled	Bow	Swordsmen	6	6-8	24-120	36-160
	Light Foot	Unprotected	Average	Undrilled	Bow	-	5	6-8	0-80	
Optional Troops									
Separately deployed veteran warriors	Medium Foot	Unprotected	Superior	Undrilled	Bow	Swordsmen	7	6-8	0-18
Skirmishers with spear-throwers	Light Foot	Unprotected	Average	Undrilled	Javelins	Light Spear	4	6-8	0-12
Subject tribe foot	Medium Foot	Unprotected	Poor	Undrilled	Bow	Swordsmen	4	6-8	0-24
	Light Foot	Unprotected	Poor	Undrilled	Bow	-	3	6-8	

AMAZONIAN FOREST TRIBE ALLIES

Troop name	Troop Type				Capabilities		Points per base	Bases per BG	Total bases
Allied commander	Field Commander/Troop Commander						40/25		1
	Type	Armour	Quality	Training	Shooting	Close Combat			
Separately deployed veterans	Medium Foot	Unprotected	Superior	Undrilled	Bow	Swordsmen	7	6	0-6
Warriors	Medium Foot	Unprotected	Average	Undrilled	Bow	Swordsmen	6	6-8	6-32	8-48
	Light Foot	Unprotected	Average	Undrilled	Bow	-	5	6-8	0-24	

TUPÍ

This list covers the cannibalistic coastal Brazilian tribes collectively known as Tupí, from 1400 to 1500 AD. These included the Tupinambá (including the Tamoyo and Ararape), the Tupinikin, Tobayara, Potiguara, Tupina, Temiminó and Caeté.

The various tribes were in a constant state of war with each other.

TROOP NOTES

The principal weapon of the Tupí was a powerful longbow made from red or black wood. Prior to the 16th century, however, their arrows were tipped with fish or animal teeth, bone or fire-hardened wood, so they did not have the armour-piercing characteristics of European longbows shooting iron or steel bodkin-headed arrows. Hence their historical effect is best represented by classification as normal Bows.

For close combat, the typical weapon was a heavy paddle-shaped club (*tacape*), once again made from red or black wood. This could be up to 1.5–1.8 metres (5–6 feet) in length, and was usually wielded with both hands. Its paddle-blade-like head had sharpened edges.

Some tribes used round or long shields as a defence against enemy arrows. Others fought without shields.

Tupí partially shaved their heads, and fought naked apart from tattoos, body paint, various brightly-coloured feather adornments, necklaces of human teeth or snail shells, and bone or white, blue or green stone lip, cheek, eyebrow, nose or ear plugs.

They preferred ambushes and surprise night attacks. Early 16th century European writers remark on their lack of discipline and disorderly mode of fighting. When a pitched battle occurred, they formed up in one large phalanx. After an exchange of arrows – during which wounded men often pulled out the arrows and continued fighting – they charged one another "like bulls" and laid about themselves with mighty blows of their two-handed clubs. Prisoners were ritually killed and eaten, sometimes after a long period of captivity.

Tupí Warriors

TUPÍ STARTER ARMY		
Commander-in-Chief	1	Field Commander
Sub-commanders	2	2 x Troop Commander
Warriors	7 BGs	Each comprising 8 bases of warriors: Average, Protected, Undrilled Medium Foot – Bow*, Heavy Weapon
Skirmishers	1 BGs	6 bases of skirmishers: Average, Unprotected, Undrilled Light Foot – Bow
Camp	1	Unfortified camp
Total	8 BGs	Camp, 62 foot bases, 3 commanders

BUILDING A CUSTOMISED LIST USING OUR ARMY POINTS

Choose an army based on the maxima and minima in the list below. The following special instructions apply to this army:

- Commanders should be depicted as warriors.
- Tupí allied commanders' contingents must conform to the Tupí allies list below, but the troops in the contingent are deducted from the minima and maxima in the main list.

Tupí warrior, by Peter Dennis.

TUPÍ

Territory Types: Tropical

C-in-C	Inspired Commander/Field Commander/Troop Commander				80/50/35		1
Sub-commanders	Field Commander/Troop Commander				50/35		0-2
Tupí allied commanders	Field Commander/Troop Commander				40/25		0-2

Troop name	Troop Type				Capabilities		Points per base	Bases per BG	Total bases
	Type	Armour	Quality	Training	Shooting	Close Combat			
Core Troops									
Warriors	Medium Foot	Protected	Average	Undrilled	Bow*	Heavy Weapon	8	6-10	30-140
		Unprotected					7		
Optional Troops									
Skirmishers	Light Foot	Unprotected	Average	Undrilled	Bow	-	5	6-8	0-12

TUPÍ ALLIES

Allied commander	Field Commander/Troop Commander				40/25		1

Troop name	Troop Type				Capabilities		Points per base	Bases per BG	Total bases
	Type	Armour	Quality	Training	Shooting	Close Combat			
Warriors	Medium Foot	Protected	Average	Undrilled	Bow*	Heavy Weapon	8	6-10	8-32
		Unprotected					7		

CHICHIMEC

The North American south-western culture was dominated by two different groups. These were the sedentary tribes of the Pueblo Culture and the nomadic Chichimec tribes. This list covers the latter group from 700 to 1500 AD.

The Chichimec tribes impacted both the American south-west and the region of Mexico. They included the Apache, the Uto-Aztecan and the Yuman.

The more settled states in what is now Mexico used the term "Chichimeca" to refer to all the nomadic tribes in the north. It carried the same connotations for them as the term "barbarian" did in Greece and Rome.

The arid lands of northern Mexico had insufficient rainfall and fertility to support widespread farming, so hunter-gathering was the norm. This occasionally led the Chichimecs into conflict with the more cultured and sedentary populations to the south but more as a local nuisance than major threat. However, a drying trend in the climate from the 12th to 14th centuries turned arid regions to desert, forcing the tribes to migrate south. That same drying trend created an opportunity as the increasing aridity caused crops to fail in the settled farming communities they were headed for.

The collapse of the Toltec trading empire followed. Trade routes could not operate effectively while disrupted by Chichimec bandits and the repeated failure of crops brought famine. The uncouth Chichimec tribes expanded into the power vacuum. Once settled in the south they formed petty states and set about casting off their past and adopting the local culture, including local religions and even getting locals to be their rulers. Anything to do with the Toltecs was adopted as "civilised".

TROOP NOTES

The main missile weapon in the earlier part of the period was the *atlatl*. Slings were also in use. Melee weapons included spears, rocks, clubs & knives. We assume that veterans would normally fight mixed in with lower-ranked warriors, but might sometimes be deployed separately.

After 900 the bow began to replace the *atlatl* and swords came to replace clubs. The bow was a major advantage in the invasion period, as it outranged the *atlatl* of the Toltecs.

16th century Spanish accounts describe Chichimec tribesmen as naked and shieldless.

CHICHIMEC STARTER ARMY (FROM 900 AD)		
Commander-in-Chief	1	Field Commander
Sub-commanders	2	2 x Troop Commander
Separately deployed veteran warriors	2 BGs	Each comprising 10 bases of separately deployed veteran warriors: Superior, Unprotected, Undrilled Medium Foot – Bow*, Light Spear, Swordsmen
Archers	2 BGs	Each comprising 10 bases of archers: Average, Unprotected, Undrilled Medium Foot – Bow*, Light Spear, Swordsmen
Skirmishing archers	6 BGs	Each comprising 6 bases of skirmishing archers: Average, Unprotected, Undrilled Light Foot - Bow
Subject tribe archers	2 BGs	Each comprising 6 bases of subject tribe archers: Poor, Unprotected, Undrilled Light Foot - Bow
Camp	1	Unfortified camp
Total	12 BGs	Camp, 88 foot bases, 3 commanders

BUILDING A CUSTOMISED LIST USING OUR ARMY POINTS

Choose an army based on the maxima and minima in the list below. The following special instructions apply to this army:

- Commanders should be depicted as veteran warriors.

- Chichimec allied commanders' contingents must conform to the Chichimec allies list below, but the troops in the contingent are deducted from the minima and maxima in the main list.

- The minimum marked * only applies before 900.

CHICHIMEC

Territory Types: Before 1250 - Desert. From 1250 – Desert, Agricultural

C-in-C	Inspired Commander/Field Commander/Troop Commander					80/50/35	1	
Sub-commanders	Field Commander/Troop Commander					50/35	0-2	
Chichimec allied commanders	Field Commander/Troop Commander					40/25	0-2	

Troop name		Troop Type				Capabilities		Points per base	Bases per BG	Total bases
		Type	Armour	Quality	Training	Shooting	Close Combat			
Core Troops										
Warriors	Only before 900	Medium Foot	Unprotected	Average	Undrilled	Javelins	Light Spear, Swordsmen	5	6-10	36-180
	Only from 900									0-32
Archers	Only from 900	Medium Foot	Unprotected	Average	Undrilled	Bow*	Light Spear, Swordsmen	6	6-10	0-56	36-180
		Medium Foot	Unprotected	Average	Undrilled	Bow	-	5	6-8	0-112
		Light Foot	Unprotected	Average	Undrilled	Bow	-	5	6-8	24-160
Atlatl skirmishers		Light Foot	Unprotected	Average	Undrilled	Javelins	Light Spear	4	6-8	*6-18
Optional Troops										
Separately deployed veteran warriors	Any date	Medium Foot	Unprotected	Superior	Undrilled	Javelins	Light Spear, Swordsmen	6	6-10	0-20
	Only from 900	Medium Foot	Unprotected	Superior	Undrilled	Bow*	Light Spear, Swordsmen	7	6-10	
Slingers		Light Foot	Unprotected	Average	Undrilled	Sling	-	4	6-8	0-16
Subject tribe archers	Only from 900	Light Foot	Unprotected	Poor	Undrilled	Bow	-	3	6-8	0-16
Other subject tribe foot		Medium Foot	Unprotected	Poor	Undrilled	-	Light Spear	2	10-12	0-12
Allies										
Pueblo Culture allies										

CHICHIMEC ALLIES

Allied commander	Field Commander/Troop Commander					40/25	1	
Troop name		Troop Type				Capabilities		Points per base	Bases per BG	Total bases
		Type	Armour	Quality	Training	Shooting	Close Combat			
Warriors	Only before 900	Medium Foot	Unprotected	Average	Undrilled	Javelins	Light Spear, Swordsmen	5	6-10	10-48
	Only from 900									0-12
Archers	Only from 900	Medium Foot	Unprotected	Average	Undrilled	Bow*	Light Spear, Swordsmen	6	6-10	0-16	10-48
		Medium Foot	Unprotected	Average	Undrilled	Bow	-	5	6-8	0-36
		Light Foot	Unprotected	Average	Undrilled	Bow	-	5	6-8	8-48
Atlatl skirmishers		Light Foot	Unprotected	Average	Undrilled	Javelins	Light Spear	4	4-6	0-6
Separately deployed veteran warriors	Any date	Medium Foot	Unprotected	Superior	Undrilled	Javelins	Light Spear, Swordsmen	6	6-8	0-8
	Only from 900	Medium Foot	Unprotected	Superior	Undrilled	Bow*	Light Spear, Swordsmen	7	6-8	
Slingers		Light Foot	Unprotected	Average	Undrilled	Sling	-	4	4-6	0-6

PUEBLO CULTURE

The Pueblo Culture of the North American south-west consisted of hunter/farmer nations dominating modern Arizona and New Mexico. Each tribe occupied rock- and plaster- palisaded towns (the pueblos), regarded as islands of stability among a sea of savage migrating tribes that flowed through the area. The Pueblo peoples included, from west to east, the Hopi, Zuni, Tewa, Tiwa, Pior, Tano and Pecos. They farmed a greater variety of crops than most other North American cultures. The defensive-minded Pueblo peoples most often defended their towns but would sometimes launch raids against neighbouring towns or nomadic tribes. Such nomadic Chichimec tribes are covered by their own list.

This list covers the Pueblo peoples from 900 to 1500 AD.

TROOP NOTES

Missile weapons included the *atlatl*, slings, bows and even a boomerang type weapon. Melee weapons included spears, rocks, clubs and knives. Some artwork shows a shield reaching from the top of a warrior's head to just above the knees. Other depictions show smaller shields reaching from the chin to the waist. By the end of the era, the round wood or hide shield became universal, with the main variation being in size.

Zuni warriors wore hardened hide armour on their head and over the torso. Zuni weapons included bow, spear and club. Shields tended to be oval.

Navajo warriors were armed with spear and bow and carried black-striped shields.

Warriors were armed with spears and a wide variety of melee weapons. We assume that veterans would normally fight mixed in with lower-ranked warriors, but might sometimes be deployed separately. Archers were massed behind shield-bearers.

PUEBLO CULTURE STARTER ARMY		
Commander-in-Chief	1	Field Commander
Sub-commanders	2	2 x Troop Commander
Separately deployed veteran warriors	2 BGs	Each comprising 8 bases of separately deployed veteran warriors: Superior, Protected, Undrilled Medium Foot – Light Spear, Swordsmen
Warriors	2 BGs	Each comprising 8 bases of warriors: Average, Protected, Undrilled Medium Foot – Light Spear, Swordsmen
Shield-bearers and archers	4 BGs	Each comprising 8 bases of shield-bearers and archers: 4 Average, Protected, Undrilled Medium Foot – Bow, Light Spear, 4 Average, Protected, Undrilled Medium Foot – Bow
Bow skirmishers	1 BG	6 bases of bow skirmishers: Average, Unprotected, Undrilled Light Foot - Bow
Slingers	1 BG	8 bases of slingers: Average, Unprotected, Undrilled Light Foot - Sling
Camp	1	Unfortified camp
Total	10 BGs	Camp, 78 foot bases, 3 commanders

Zuni warrior, by Peter Dennis.

BUILDING A CUSTOMISED LIST USING OUR ARMY POINTS

Choose an army based on the maxima and minima in the list below. The following special instructions apply to this army:

- Commanders should be depicted as veteran warriors.
- Pueblo Culture allied commanders' contingents must conform to the Pueblo Culture allies list below, but the troops in the contingent are deducted from the minima and maxima in the main list.

66

PUEBLO CULTURE

Territory Types: Desert, Agricultural

C-in-C		Inspired Commander/Field Commander/Troop Commander				80/50/35		1	
Sub-commanders		Field Commander/Troop Commander				50/35		0-2	
Pueblo Culture allied commanders		Field Commander/Troop Commander				40/25		0-2	

Troop name		Troop Type				Capabilities		Points per base	Bases per BG	Total bases
		Type	Armour	Quality	Training	Shooting	Close Combat			
Core Troops										
Warriors	Zuni	Medium Foot	Protected	Average	Undrilled	-	Light Spear, Swordsmen	6	6-10	12-60
	Others	Medium Foot	Protected	Average	Undrilled	-	Light Spear, Swordsmen	6	6-10	
			Unprotected					5		
Shield-bearers and archers		Medium Foot	Protected	Average	Undrilled	Bow	Light Spear	6	1/2 6-8	24-80
		Medium Foot	Protected	Average	Undrilled	Bow	-	6	1/2	
Bow skirmishers		Light Foot	Unprotected	Average	Undrilled	Bow	-	5	6-8	6-24
Optional Troops										
Separately deployed veteran warriors		Medium Foot	Protected	Superior	Undrilled	-	Light Spear, Swordsmen	8	6-8	0-18
Atlatl skirmishers		Light Foot	Unprotected	Average	Undrilled	Javelins	Light Spear	4	6-8	0-16
Slingers		Light Foot	Unprotected	Average	Undrilled	Sling	-	4	6-8	0-16
Villagers		Mob	Unprotected	Poor	Undrilled	-	-	2	6-10	0-10
Allies										
Chichimec allies										

PUEBLO CULTURE ALLIES

Allied commander		Field Commander/Troop Commander				40/25		1		
Troop name		Troop Type				Capabilities		Points per base	Bases per BG	Total bases
		Type	Armour	Quality	Training	Shooting	Close Combat			
Separately deployed veteran warriors		Medium Foot	Protected	Superior	Undrilled	-	Light Spear, Swordsmen	8	4-6	0-6
Warriors	Zuni	Medium Foot	Protected	Average	Undrilled	-	Light Spear, Swordsmen	6	6-10	6-18
	Others	Medium Foot	Protected	Average	Undrilled	-	Light Spear, Swordsmen	6	6-10	
			Unprotected					5		
Shield-bearers and archers		Medium Foot	Protected	Average	Undrilled	Bow	Light Spear	6	1/2 6-8	8-24
		Medium Foot	Protected	Average	Undrilled	Bow	-	6	1/2	
Bow skirmishers		Light Foot	Unprotected	Average	Undrilled	Bow	-	5	6-8	0-8
Atlatl skirmishers		Light Foot	Unprotected	Average	Undrilled	Javelins	Light Spear	4	4-6	0-6 / 4-16
Slingers		Light Foot	Unprotected	Average	Undrilled	Sling	-	4	4-6	0-6

MOUND-BUILDER CULTURE

The term Mound-Builder refers to the sedentary native North American cultures who constructed various styles of earthen mounds for residential, ceremonial and burial purposes. Such sedentary cultures were marked by permanent towns protected by palisades. At various times they came under attack by migrating waves of new tribes entering the region.

There were primitive mounds and towns as far back as 2500 BC. The more organised Mound-

Builder culture with formal societal hierarchies and central armouries began as early as 1000 BC but reached its height in about 1000 AD. After that time, other south-eastern tribes began to compete for dominance.

The initial Mound-Builder phase is called the Adena phase (400 BC–200 AD). This co-existed with and was then superseded by the Hopewell phase (100 BC–500 AD). Both of these cultures were based in the Ohio valley and the southern coast of the Great Lakes. In the south it is called the Mississippian Culture (700 AD–1500 AD), as the primary towns were located along the Mississippi River. A few minor regional Mound-Builder cultures could be found in Georgia, Florida and elsewhere.

From c.1300 in the south the Mound-Builder culture co-existed with the South-Eastern Woodland culture.

The Natchez are an example of a late Mound-Builder culture, occupying, in 1500, an area east of the Mississippi river in modern Mississippi. They had an interesting hierarchical social system involving exogamous marriage. The noble class was divided into "Suns" (chieftains), "Nobles" and "Honoured" people. The "Suns", at least, were required to marry commoners – "Stinkards", probably to prevent the genetic effects of consanguineous marriages. If their mother was noble, the children of such marriages retained their mothers' status, while if the father was noble the children dropped one social class from that of their father. When a male "Sun" died, his wives were expected to commit ritual suicide, and often several of his closest followers did so too.

At the time of the arrival of the French in the late 17th century, the Natchez were ruled by a paramount chief, the "Great Sun", who controlled civil affairs, and his brother, the "Tattooed Serpent", who controlled foreign relations and war. The "Great Sun" was borne on a litter, so that his feet would not be defiled by touching the ground.

The list covers the Mound-Builder culture from 900 to 1500 AD.

TROOP NOTES

Early warriors used the *atlatl*. By 900 AD, the bow and arrow had been perfected and was in common use. The single-handed war-club was the commonest close-quarters weapon. De Soto's men reported central armouries consisting of shields, long spears, bows, and war-clubs among other items. As might be expected, the higher caste warriors received better shields and arms than the lower castes.

Subject foot represent vassal tribes. Allied contingents are from neighbouring Mound-Builder towns.

The "Great Sun" in his litter could be represented as part of the camp.

Mound Builder
Foot

MOUND-BUILDER STARTER ARMY

Commander-in-Chief	1	Field Commander
Sub-commanders	2	2 x Troop Commander
Nobles and retainers	3 BGs	Each comprising 6 bases of nobles and retainers: Superior, Protected, Undrilled Medium Foot – Bow*, Light Spear, Swordsmen
Honoured men	4 BGs	Each comprising 8 bases of honoured men: Average, Protected, Undrilled Medium Foot – Bow*, Light Spear, Swordsmen
Stinkard archers	3 BGs	Each comprising 6 bases of stinkard archers: Poor, Unprotected, Undrilled Light Foot - Bow
Other stinkard foot	2 BGs	Each comprising 10 bases of other stinkard foot: Poor, Unprotected, Undrilled, Medium Foot – Light Spear
Camp	1	Unfortified camp
Total	12 BGs	Camp, 88 foot bases, 3 commanders

Mississippian warrior, by Peter Dennis.

Mound Builder priests (standing) and tribespeople, by Richard Hook. Taken from Men-at-Arms 288: American Indians of the Southeast.

BUILDING A CUSTOMISED LIST USING OUR ARMY POINTS

Choose an army based on the maxima and minima in the list below. The following special instructions apply to this army:

- Commanders should be depicted as nobles.
- Mound-Builder allied commanders' contingents must conform to the Mound-Builder allies list below, but the troops in the contingent are deducted from the minima and maxima in the main list.

MOUND-BUILDER CULTURE

Territory Types: Woodlands, Agricultural

C-in-C	Inspired Commander/Field Commander/Troop Commander						80/50/35	1	
Sub-commanders	Field Commander						50	0-2	
	Troop Commander						35	0-3	
Mound-Builder allied commanders	Field Commander/Troop Commander						40/25	0-2	
Troop name	Troop Type				Capabilities		Points per base	Bases per BG	Total bases
	Type	Armour	Quality	Training	Shooting	Close Combat			
Core Troops									
Nobles and retainers	Medium Foot	Protected	Superior	Undrilled	Bow*	Light Spear, Swordsmen	9	6-8	6-18
Honoured men	Medium Foot	Protected	Average	Undrilled	Bow*	Light Spear, Swordsmen	7	6-8	12-84
Subject tribe or stinkard archers	Medium Foot	Unprotected	Poor	Undrilled	Bow	Light Spear	3	8	8-64
	Light Foot	Unprotected	Poor	Undrilled	Bow	-	3	8	
Other subject tribe or stinkard foot	Medium Foot	Unprotected	Poor	Undrilled	-	Light Spear	2	12	12-72
Optional Troops									
Ambushers or skirmishers	Light Foot	Unprotected	Average	Undrilled	Javelins	Light Spear	4	6-8	0-16

MOUND-BUILDER ALLIES

Allied commander	Field Commander/Troop Commander						40/25	1	
Troop name	Troop Type				Capabilities		Points per base	Bases per BG	Total bases
	Type	Armour	Quality	Training	Shooting	Close Combat			
Nobles and retainers	Medium Foot	Protected	Superior	Undrilled	Bow*	Light Spear, Swordsmen	9	4-6	4-6
Honoured men	Medium Foot	Protected	Average	Undrilled	Bow*	Light Spear, Swordsmen	7	6-8	6-24
Stinkard archers	Medium Foot	Unprotected	Poor	Undrilled	Bow	Light Spear	3	8	0-16
	Light Foot	Unprotected	Poor	Undrilled	Bow	-	3	8	
Other stinkard foot	Medium Foot	Unprotected	Poor	Undrilled	-	Light Spear	2	12	0-24
Ambushers or skirmishers	Light Foot	Unprotected	Average	Undrilled	Javelins	Light Spear	4	4-6	0-6

Mississippian chunkey players, Birdman dancer and priest, by Richard Hook. Taken from Men-at-Arms 288: American Indians of the Southeast.

SOUTH-EASTERN WOODLAND CULTURE

The South-Eastern Woodland culture was a post-Mound-Builder culture that dominated the south-east of the modern United States until the arrival of Europeans. The tribes were from various language/cultural groups, including the Caddo, Biloxi-Souian, Timucuan and the dominant Muskogee. Also located among the various tribes were tribes who were still associated with the Mound-Builder culture, such as the Natchez, who are covered by the Mound-Builder culture list.

At the start of the 1500s, the Muskogee occupied nearly all of what is now the south-east United States. The Muskogee culture consisted of the Creek, Choctaw, Hitchiti-Creek, and Muskogee-Creek. The other dominant tribe which entered the area at the end of the era was the Cherokee, who were Iroquoian.

The Creek nation operated as a loose confederacy with minor tribes from different ethnic groups. This confederation is thought to have started as a defensive strategy against the other larger Indian tribes of the region. The Creek alliance would gain and lose land and people as small tribes joined and withdrew. The Creek towns were located mainly in the modern states of Georgia and Alabama.

The Choctaw were the largest of the Muskogean culture nations. They controlled the area of middle and southern Mississippi, with some villages and hunting territory located east of Tombigbee River. They were closely related to the Chickasaw, who were their bitter enemies. The Choctaw were differentiated from other Muskogean tribes by the practice of "head flattening" and wearing long and unbraided hair.

The Chickasaw was another Muskogean tribe, closely related to the Choctaw in language and customs. The Chickasaw initially settled in northern Alabama on the north side of the Tennessee River. Eventually they established their main towns in northern Mississippi. The warlike Chickasaw claimed hunting territory far from their villages. They were constantly fighting with the nearby tribes, including the Choctaw, Creeks, Cherokee, Illinois, Kickapoo, Shawnee, Mobilians, Osage, and Quapaw.

This list covers armies of the South-Eastern Woodland culture from 1300 to 1500 AD.

TROOP NOTES

Warriors include a mixture of veteran and lower ranking warriors variously armed with bows and/or spears and/or war-clubs. Veteran warriors can be distinguished by warriors using two-hand war-clubs or by wearing gorgets of shell. Ambush parties were assigned at the initial war councils and comprised picked warriors.

Some use was made of raw-hide armour and shields. The extent of such usage is uncertain. We therefore give the option of rating troops as Protected or Unprotected.

The Pensacola Bay and Mobile Bay Choctaws used *atlatls* instead of bows.

Subject tribes are vassals of the dominant tribe in the area.

SOUTH-EAST WOODLAND STARTER ARMY

Commander-in-Chief	1	Field Commander
Sub-commanders	2	2 x Troop Commander
Veteran warriors	1 BG	6 bases of veteran warriors: Superior, Protected, Undrilled Medium Foot – Heavy Weapon
Ambush parties	2 BGs	Each comprising 6 bases of ambush parties: Superior, Protected, Undrilled Medium Foot – Bow*, Impact Foot, Swordsmen
Warriors	3 BGs	Each comprising 8 bases of warriors: Average, Protected, Undrilled Medium Foot – Bow*, Impact Foot, Swordsmen
Skirmishing archers	3 BGs	Each comprising 6 bases of skirmishing archers: Average, Unprotected, Undrilled Light Foot - Bow
Subject tribe foot	1 BG	12 bases of subject tribe foot: Poor, Unprotected, Undrilled, Medium Foot – Light Spear
Camp	1	Unfortified camp
Total	10 BGs	Camp, 72 foot bases, 3 commanders

BUILDING A CUSTOMISED LIST USING OUR ARMY POINTS

Choose an army based on the maxima and minima in the list below. The following special instructions apply to this army:

- Commanders should be depicted as veteran warriors.

- South-Eastern Woodland allied commanders' contingents must conform to the South-Eastern Woodland allies list below, but the troops in the contingent are deducted from the minima and maxima in the main list. Choctaws can have non-Choctaw allies and vice versa.

SOUTH-EASTERN WOODLAND CULTURE

Territory Types: Woodlands, Hills, Agricultural

C-in-C		Inspired Commander/Field Commander/Troop Commander						80/50/35		1
Sub-commanders		Field Commander						50		0-2
		Troop Commander						35		0-3
South-Eastern Woodland allied commanders		Field Commander/Troop Commander						40/25		0-2

Troop name		Troop Type				Capabilities		Points per base	Bases per BG	Total bases
		Type	Armour	Quality	Training	Shooting	Close Combat			
Core Troops										
Separately deployed veteran warriors or ambush parties	Any	Medium Foot	Protected	Superior	Undrilled	–	Heavy Weapon	9	6-10	6-20
			Unprotected					7		
	Any except Pensacola or Mobile Bay Choctaws	Medium Foot	Protected	Superior	Undrilled	Bow*	Impact Foot, Swordsmen	10	6-10	
			Unprotected					8		
	Only Pensacola or Mobile Bay Choctaws	Medium Foot	Protected	Superior	Undrilled	Javelins	Impact Foot, Swordsmen	9	6-10	
			Unprotected					7		
Warriors	Any except Pensacola or Mobile Bay Choctaws	Medium Foot	Protected	Average	Undrilled	Bow*	Impact Foot, Swordsmen	8	8-10	24-120
			Unprotected					7		
	Only Pensacola or Mobile Bay Choctaws	Medium Foot	Protected	Average	Undrilled	Javelins	Impact Foot, Swordsmen	7	8-10	
			Unprotected					6		

Optional Troops										
Skirmishing archers	Any except Pensacola or Mobile Bay Choctaws	Light Foot	Unprotected	Average	Undrilled	Bow	-	5	6-8	0-24
Atlatl skirmishers	Only Pensacola or Mobile Bay Choctaws	Light Foot	Unprotected	Average	Undrilled	Javelins	Light Spear	4	6-8	
Subject tribe foot		Medium Foot	Unprotected	Poor	Undrilled	-	Light Spear	2	10-12	0-24

SOUTH-EASTERN WOODLAND ALLIES

Allied commander		Field Commander/Troop Commander						40/25		1
Troop name		Troop Type				Capabilities		Points per base	Bases per BG	Total bases
		Type	Armour	Quality	Training	Shooting	Close Combat			
Separately deployed veteran warriors or ambush parties	Any	Medium Foot	Protected	Superior	Undrilled	-	Heavy Weapon	9	6-8	0-8
			Unprotected					7		
	Any except Pensacola or Mobile Bay Choctaws	Medium Foot	Protected	Superior	Undrilled	Bow*	Impact Foot, Swordsmen	10	6-8	
			Unprotected					8		
	Only Pensacola or Mobile Bay Choctaws	Medium Foot	Protected	Superior	Undrilled	Javelins	Impact Foot, Swordsmen	9	6-8	
			Unprotected					7		
Warriors	Any except Pensacola or Mobile Bay Choctaws	Medium Foot	Protected	Average	Undrilled	Bow*	Impact Foot, Swordsmen	8	8-10	8-32
			Unprotected					7		
	Only Pensacola or Mobile Bay Choctaws	Medium Foot	Protected	Average	Undrilled	Javelins	Impact Foot, Swordsmen	7	8-10	
			Unprotected					6		
Skirmishing archers	Any except Pensacola or Mobile Bay Choctaws	Light Foot	Unprotected	Average	Undrilled	Bow	-	5	6-8	0-8
Atlatl skirmishers	Only Pensacola or Mobile Bay Choctaws	Light Foot	Unprotected	Average	Undrilled	Javelins	Light Spear	4	6-8	

TIMUCUAN

The Timucuans lived in what is now northern Florida and south-east Georgia. They lived in palisaded villages and practiced agriculture, hunting and fishing. They are regarded as being part of the South-Eastern Woodland culture but their military practices developed into a more formal use of formations. This list is based primarily on the wood carvings made by French allies of the Timucuan forces who fought with the French against tribes allied with the Spanish. These date from after the end of our period, but there is no reason to suppose that there had been any changes from earlier times.

This list covers Timucuan armies from 1200 to 1500 AD.

TROOP NOTES

Timucuan troops are shown in French wood-carvings marching in step in hollow square formation. It is possible that this may merely be artistic convention, but we give the option of classifying them as Drilled. The front of the

formation consisted of masses of archers whose task it was to pin the enemy in place. The flanks of the formation consisted of men with multi-barbed spears who would rush out to extend past the enemy's flank. The rear wall consisted of more warriors whose mission was to reinforce the archers or rush to a weak flank.

Warriors used a mixture of spears and large paddle-shaped two-handed wooden clubs. Battle groups rated as Heavy Weapon are those with a higher proportion of men with clubs. Battle groups rated as Light Spear, Swordsmen are those with a higher proportion of spearmen. We assume

that veterans would normally fight mixed in with lower-ranked warriors, but might sometimes be deployed separately.

Shields are shown in some depictions, as are wicker helmets and copper or shell pectorals. It is not known what proportion of men were so equipped. We therefore give Protected and Unprotected options.

Depictions show archers stabbing at enemy warriors with what appear to be long cane arrows. This may possibly justify Light Spear capability.

Javelins had fish bone or shell edge points.

Subject troops are allies from smaller towns.

TIMUCUAN STARTER ARMY		
Commander-in-Chief	1	Field Commander
Sub-commanders	2	2 x Troop Commander
Separately deployed veteran warriors	2 BGs	Each comprising 8 bases of separately veteran warriors: Superior, Unprotected, Drilled Medium Foot – Heavy Weapon
Warriors	1 BG	10 bases of warriors: Average, Unprotected, Drilled Medium Foot – Heavy Weapon
Warriors	2 BGs	Each comprising 8 bases of warriors: Average, Protected, Drilled Medium Foot – Light Spear, Swordsmen
Archers	2 BGs	Each comprising 8 bases of archers: Average, Unprotected, Drilled Medium Foot – Bow, Light Spear
Javelin skirmishers	2 BGs	Each comprising 6 bases of javelin skirmishers: Average, Unprotected, Undrilled Light Foot – Javelins, Light Spear
Subject tribe archers	1 BG	8 bases of subject tribe archers: Poor, Unprotected, Undrilled Light Foot - Bow
Camp	1	Unfortified camp
Total	10 BGs	Camp, 78 foot bases, 3 commanders

BUILDING A CUSTOMISED LIST USING OUR ARMY POINTS

Choose an army based on the maxima and minima in the list below. The following special instructions apply to this army:

- Commanders should be depicted as veteran warriors.
- If any troops are rated as Drilled, all troops with that option must be so rated.

TIMUCUAN

Territory Types: Tropical, Woodland, Agricultural

C-in-C	Inspired Commander/Field Commander/Troop Commander			80/50/35	1	
Sub-commanders	Field Commander			50	0-2	
	Troop Commander			35	0-3	

Troop name	Troop Type				Capabilities		Points per base	Bases per BG	Total bases
	Type	Armour	Quality	Training	Shooting	Close Combat			
Core Troops									
Archers	Medium Foot	Unprotected	Average	Drilled	Bow	-	6	6-8	12-48
				Undrilled			5		
	Medium Foot	Unprotected	Average	Drilled	Bow	Light Spear	6	6-8	
				Undrilled			5		
Warriors	Medium Foot	Protected	Average	Drilled	-	Light Spear, Swordsmen	7	6-10	12-72
		Protected		Undrilled			6		
		Unprotected		Drilled			6		
		Unprotected		Undrilled			5		
	Medium Foot	Protected	Average	Drilled	-	Heavy Weapon	8	6-10	
		Protected		Undrilled			7		
		Unprotected		Drilled			7		
		Unprotected		Undrilled			6		
Javelin skirmishers	Light Foot	Unprotected	Average	Undrilled	Javelins	Light Spear	4	6-8	6-16
Optional Troops									
Separately deployed veteran warriors	Medium Foot	Protected	Superior	Drilled	-	Light Spear, Swordsmen	9	6-8	0-18
		Protected		Undrilled			8		
		Unprotected		Drilled			7		
		Unprotected		Undrilled			6		
	Medium Foot	Protected	Superior	Drilled	-	Heavy Weapon	10	6-8	
		Protected		Undrilled			9		
		Unprotected		Drilled			8		
		Unprotected		Undrilled			7		
Subject tribe archers	Medium Foot	Unprotected	Poor	Undrilled	Bow	Light Spear	3	6-8	0-12
	Light Foot	Unprotected	Poor	Undrilled	Bow	-	3	6-8	
Subject tribe javelin skirmishers	Light Foot	Unprotected	Poor	Undrilled	Javelins	Light Spear	2	6-8	0-8
Other subject tribe foot	Medium Foot	Unprotected	Poor	Undrilled	-	Light Spear	2	10-12	0-24
Allies									
South-Eastern Woodland allies									

EASTERN WOODLAND CULTURE

The dominant language groups among the North American Eastern Woodland culture were the Iroquois and the Algonquin.

The Algonquian tribes were living in the region first in about 700 AD. Several Algonquian tribes were called Abenaki. Abenaki is a geographical and linguistic term rather than a specific tribal name. Before European contact individual tribes were independent. Occasionally several tribes would unite under a powerful chieftain (*sachem*) for purposes of war.

Field Commander

The Iroquois entered the area in about 1100. The individual Iroquoian tribes were divided into three clans – Turtle, Bear, and Wolf – each headed by the clan mother. The Iroquoian tribes were known for operating in confederacies of related tribes. The various Iroquoian confederacies (Neutrals, Susquehannock, Huron and New York Iroquois) were established prior to European contact. The Huron of southern Canada and the Susquehannock of modern Pennsylvania were frequently at war with the New York Iroquois.

This list covers Eastern Woodland culture armies from 900 to 1500 AD.

TROOP NOTES

After their first military encounters with the Iroquois, the French described some Iroquois warriors as fighting in a very close wedge formation, armed with a mixture of one-handed and two-handed war-clubs and wearing a form of wooden body armour. We assume these represent the most experienced warriors. One-handed clubs predominated.

Common warriors fought in fairly dense but mobile formations, and were armed with mixed melee weapons and/or bows. Large shields are depicted by European observers.

Iroquois Warrior

IROQUOIS STARTER ARMY		
Commander-in-Chief	1	Field Commander
Sub-commanders	2	2 x Troop Commander
Separately deployed veteran warriors	2 BGs	Each comprising 8 bases of separately deployed veteran warriors: Superior, Protected, Undrilled Heavy Foot – Impact Foot, Swordsmen
Warriors	4 BGs	Each comprising 8 bases of warriors: Average, Protected, Undrilled Medium Foot – Bow*, Impact Foot, Swordsmen
Skirmishers	1 BG	6 bases of skirmishers: Average, Unprotected, Undrilled Light Foot – Javelins, Light Spear
Subject tribe archers	3 BGs	Each comprising 6 bases of subject tribe archers: Poor, Unprotected, Undrilled Light Foot - Bow
Camp	1	Unfortified camp
Total	10 BGs	Camp, 72 foot bases, 3 commanders

BUILDING A CUSTOMISED LIST USING OUR ARMY POINTS

Choose an army based on the maxima and minima in the list below. The following special instructions apply to this army:

- Commanders should be depicted as veteran warriors.
- Separately deployed veteran warriors can be graded as Heavy Foot or Medium Foot but all separately deployed veteran warriors of the same tribe must be graded the same. Those of allied tribes can be graded differently.
- Eastern Woodland allied commanders' contingents must conform to the Eastern Woodland allies list below, but the troops in the contingent are deducted from the minima and maxima in the main list.

Early New England tribespeople, by Jonathan Smith. Taken from Men-at-Arms 428:
Indian Tribes of the New England Frontier.

Early Iroquois leaders, by Jonathan Smith. Taken from Men-at-Arms 395:
Tribes of the Iroquois Confederacy.

EASTERN WOODLAND CULTURE

Territory Types: Woodland, Hilly, Agricultural

C-in-C	Inspired Commander/Field Commander/Troop Commander						80/50/35		1
Sub-commanders	Field Commander						50		0-2
	Troop Commander						35		0-3
Eastern Woodland allied commanders	Field Commander/Troop Commander						40/25		0-2

Troop name	Troop Type				Capabilities		Points per base	Bases per BG	Total bases
	Type	Armour	Quality	Training	Shooting	Close Combat			
Core Troops									
Separately deployed veteran warriors	Heavy Foot or Medium Foot	Protected	Superior	Undrilled	-	Impact Foot, Swordsmen	9	6-8	6-24
Warriors	Medium Foot	Protected	Average	Undrilled	Bow*	Impact Foot, Swordsmen	8	8-10	20-96
		Unprotected					7		
Skirmishers	Light Foot	Unprotected	Average	Undrilled	Javelins	Light Spear	4	6-8	6-24
	Light Foot	Unprotected	Average	Undrilled	Bow	-	5	6-8	
Optional Troops									
Subject tribe archers	Light Foot	Unprotected	Poor	Undrilled	Bow	-	3	6-8	0-24
Other subject tribe foot	Medium Foot	Unprotected	Poor	Undrilled	-	Light Spear	2	10-12	0-20

EASTERN WOODLAND ALLIES

Allied commander	Field Commander/Troop Commander						40/25		1

Troop name	Troop Type				Capabilities		Points per base	Bases per BG	Total bases
	Type	Armour	Quality	Training	Shooting	Close Combat			
Separately deployed veteran warriors	Heavy Foot or Medium Foot	Protected	Superior	Undrilled	-	Impact Foot, Swordsmen	9	6-8	0-8
Warriors	Medium Foot	Protected	Average	Undrilled	Bow*	Impact Foot, Swordsmen	8	8-10	8-32
		Unprotected					7		
Skirmishers	Light Foot	Unprotected	Average	Undrilled	Javelins	Light Spear	4	6-8	0-8
	Light Foot	Unprotected	Average	Undrilled	Bow	-	5	6-8	

PLAINS CULTURE

Plains Culture tribes covered the largest area of any of the pre-Columbian North American cultures. Some of the languages included in this culture were Souian, Caddoan, and Shoshonean.

Most of the Plains tribes had been driven westward from the North-Eastern Woodlands region by other tribes. The Comanche and Kiowa were driven out onto the plains from the Rockies by other Great Basin tribes. The other plains tribes included the Lakota/Sioux, Assiniboine, Crow, Blackfeet, Arapaho, Cheyenne, and Gros Ventre.

In the pre-Columbian era, there was a mixture of sedentary and nomadic tribes. The sedentary tribes built palisaded towns along rivers and on lakes. They practiced agriculture, pottery, and simple weaving. The nomadic tribes migrated constantly, used tipis for housing, and hunted the buffalo (American bison) as their primary source of food.

This list covers Plains tribe armies from 900 to 1500 AD.

TROOP NOTES

The armies of the pre-horse era comprised large masses of foot warriors armed with a variety of weapons and carrying large shields. Spears were common and varied in length from tribe to tribe. Other close combat weapons included mace-shaped clubs and hand hatchets. The Assiniboine used a club consisting of a two pound stone in a hide bag attached to a wooden handle by sinew cords. The Cree version consisted of the stone and bag but was attached loosely to the 0.6 metre (2 feet) handle so it could sway to give more momentum – giving a similar effect to a medieval flail. Cree "flail" men battle groups represent groups with a high proportion of men so-armed.

Bows were also common. They were especially important in Texas and along the Gulf Coast.

After softening up the enemy with arrows and javelins, one force would rush the other in a massive wave, hoping to overwhelm them.

Weapons were made of wood, stone and bone. Stone weapons included arrow heads, lance heads, knives, axes, and club heads. Bone tended to be used to enhance weapons such as knives and arrow points. Long spears were common. A few tribes are credited with using poisoned arrows.

Both shields and bows were larger in the Pre-Columbian era than later. Shields were made of buffalo hide with protection extending from chin to mid-calf. The Blackfoot have traditions of having protected themselves from arrows by several skin shirts, one over the other, while the Northern Shoshoni wore armour comprised of "many folds of dressed antelope skin united with glue and sand." The Pawnee have also been credited with hardened skin coats. Since armour and helmets were used in some parts of the north Pacific Coast area and in parts of the Plateaus, it is natural to encounter armour on the north-western margin of the Plains.

CREE STARTER ARMY		
Commander-in-Chief	1	Troop Commander
Sub-commanders	2	2 x Troop Commander
"Flail" men	2 BGs	Each comprising 8 bases of "flail" men: Average, Protected, Undrilled Medium Foot – Heavy Weapon
Warriors and archers	4 BGs	Each comprising 8 bases of warriors and archers: Average, Protected, Undrilled Medium Foot – Bow*, Impact Foot, Swordsmen
Skirmishing archers	4 BGs	Each comprising 6 bases of archers: Average, Unprotected, Undrilled Light Foot – Bow
Camp	1	Unfortified camp
Total	10 BGs	Camp, 72 foot bases, 3 commanders

BUILDING A CUSTOMISED LIST USING OUR ARMY POINTS

Choose an army based on the maxima and minima in the list below. The following special instructions apply to this army:

- Commanders should be depicted as warriors.

- Plains Tribe allied commanders' contingents must conform to the Plains Culture allies list below, but the troops in the contingent are deducted from the minima and maxima in the main list.

- The minima marked * only apply if mixed bodies of warriors and archers are not used. The minimum marked ** applies if they are.

PLAINS CULTURE

Territory Types: Steppe, Agricultural

C-in-C	Inspired Commander/Field Commander/Troop Commander				80/50/35		1	
Sub-commanders	Field Commander/Troop Commander				50/35		0-2	
Plains Tribe allied commanders	Field Commander/Troop Commander				40/25		0-2	

Troop name	Troop Type				Capabilities		Points per base	Bases per BG	Total bases
	Type	Armour	Quality	Training	Shooting	Close Combat			
Core Troops									
Warriors	Medium Foot	Protected	Average	Undrilled	-	Impact Foot, Swordsmen	7	8-12	*16-120
Mixed bodies of warriors and archers	Medium Foot	Protected	Average	Undrilled	Bow*	Impact Foot, Swordsmen	8	8-12	**24-144	24-184
Archers	Light Foot	Unprotected	Average	Undrilled	Bow	-	5	6-8	*8-64
Optional Troops									
"Flail" men	Only Cree	Medium Foot	Protected	Average	Undrilled	Heavy Weapon	7	6-8	0-16

PLAINS CULTURE ALLIES

Allied commander	Field Commander/Troop Commander				40/25		1	
Troop name	Troop Type				Capabilities		Points per base	Bases per BG	Total bases
	Type	Armour	Quality	Training	Shooting	Close Combat			
Warriors	Medium Foot	Protected	Average	Undrilled	-	Impact Foot, Swordsmen	7	8-12	*8-36
Mixed bodies of warriors and archers	Medium Foot	Protected	Average	Undrilled	Bow*	Impact Foot, Swordsmen	8	8-12	**8-40	8-48
Archers	Light Foot	Unprotected	Average	Undrilled	Bow	-	5	6-8	*6-18
"Flail" men	Only Cree	Medium Foot	Protected	Average	Undrilled	-	Heavy Weapon	7	4-6	0-6

PACIFIC NORTH-WEST CULTURE

This list covers the geographic areas known as the Mackenzie, the North-West Coast, the California Basin and the Plateau, comprising numerous language groups, each with its own cultural variation. The dominant nations in the Pacific North-West were the Athapascan, Tlingit and Salishan. The Salishan, in particular, influenced the neighbouring regions with incursions and later migrations.

The North-Western tribes mainly lived in towns and maintained a sedentary lifestyle which relied heavily on fishing. Houses were constructed of cedar planks. Canoes were dug out from cedar, redwood in the south, and some were ocean-going. The tribes were active traders and most practiced slavery and headhunting.

Tlingit Village with defenders

This list covers the North-Western cultures from 1100 to 1500 AD.

TROOP NOTES

The main weapons were bows, heavy one-handed clubs, wedge-shaped double-bladed daggers (designed to penetrate body armour), short heavy thrusting spears and a few slings. Slings were more common in the far north due in part to difficulty in making and maintaining strong bows and arrows in northern conditions. Aleuts used darts.

As shields were not generally used, a rush with a club in one hand and the double-bladed dagger in the other was a common tactic. Scalps were not taken – severed heads were the preferred trophy, displayed in front of the victorious warrior's house.

While shields were rare, body armour was common. In the Mackenzie region cuirasses and cloaks of elk and moose skin were used or strips of hide were used to cover the warrior from his armpit to his hip. In the Pacific North-West area, body armour was made from rod-reeds, and was very effective against arrows. Also popular among the Tlingit, Haida and Tsimshian nations were elaborately carved wooden helmets that covered the entire head and face.

Totem-men were the highest ranking veteran warriors – they wore wooden body armour and wooden protective masks/helmets representing different animals. Lesser veterans wore protective wooden armour but no masks, as they had not yet reached that status. We assume that veterans would normally fight mixed in with lower-ranked warriors, but might sometimes be deployed separately.

Subject foot represent masses of vassal or subject tribesmen with mixed weapons and little motivation.

Tlingit Warriors

PACIFIC NORTH-WEST CULTURE STARTER ARMY		
Commander-in-Chief	1	Field Commander
Sub-commanders	2	2 x Troop Commander
Separately deployed totem-men and other veterans	2 BGs	Each comprising 8 bases of separately deployed totem-men and other veterans: Superior, Protected, Undrilled Medium Foot – Impact Foot, Swordsmen
Warriors	3 BGs	Each comprising 8 bases of warriors: Average, Protected, Undrilled Medium Foot – Bow*, Impact Foot, Swordsmen
Skirmishers	4 BGs	Each comprising 6 bases of skirmishers: Average, Unprotected, Undrilled Light Foot – Bow
Subject foot	1 BG	12 bases of subject foot: Poor, Unprotected, Undrilled Medium Foot – Light Spear
Camp	1	Unfortified camp
Total	10 BGs	Camp, 76 foot bases, 3 commanders

Makah whaler (left), Cowichan (centre) and Kwakiutl (right) warriors, by Christa Hook.
Taken from Men-at-Arms 418: American Indians of the Pacific Northwest.

BUILDING A CUSTOMISED LIST USING OUR ARMY POINTS

Choose an army based on the maxima and minima in the list below. The following special instructions apply to this army:

- Commanders should be depicted as totem-men.
- Pacific North-West allied commanders' contingents must conform to the Pacific North-West allies list below, but the troops in the contingent are deducted from the minima and maxima in the main list.

PACIFIC NORTH-WEST CULTURE

Territory Types: Hilly, Agricultural, Woodland

C-in-C	Inspired Commander/Field Commander/Troop Commander						80/50/35		1	
Sub-commanders	Field Commander						50		0-2	
	Troop Commander						35		0-3	
Pacific North-West allied commanders	Field Commander/Troop Commander						40/25		0-2	

Troop name	Troop Type				Capabilities		Points per base	Bases per BG	Total bases	
	Type	Armour	Quality	Training	Shooting	Close Combat				
Core Troops										
Warriors	Medium Foot	Protected	Average	Undrilled	Bow*	Impact Foot, Swordsmen	8	8-10	24-100	
		Unprotected					7			
Skirmishers	Any tribe	Light Foot	Unprotected	Average	Undrilled	Javelins	Light Spear	4	6-8	0-24	6-24
		Light Foot	Unprotected	Average	Undrilled	Bow	-	5	6-8		
	Only far northern tribes	Light Foot	Unprotected	Average	Undrilled	Sling	-	4	6-8	0-18	
Optional Troops										
Separately deployed totem-men and other veterans	Medium Foot	Protected	Superior	Undrilled	-	Impact Foot, Swordsmen	9	6-8	0-32	
Subject foot	Mob	Unprotected	Poor	Undrilled	-	Light Spear	2	10-12	0-24	

PACIFIC NORTH-WEST ALLIES

Allied commander	Field Commander/Troop Commander						40/25		1	
Troop name	Troop Type				Capabilities		Points per base	Bases per BG	Total bases	
	Type	Armour	Quality	Training	Shooting	Close Combat				
Separately deployed totem-men and other veterans	Medium Foot	Protected	Superior	Undrilled	-	Impact Foot, Swordsmen	9	6-8	0-12	
Warriors	Medium Foot	Protected	Average	Undrilled	Bow*	Impact Foot, Swordsmen	8	8-10	8-32	
		Unprotected					7			
Skirmishers	Any tribe	Light Foot	Unprotected	Average	Undrilled	Javelins	Light Spear	4	6-8	0-8	0-8
		Light Foot	Unprotected	Average	Undrilled	Bow	-	5	6-8		
	Only far northern tribes	Light Foot	Unprotected	Average	Undrilled	Sling	-	4	4-6	0-6	

APPENDIX 1 – USING THE LISTS

To give balanced games, armies can be selected using the points system. The more effective the troops, the more each base costs in points. The maximum points for an army will usually be set at between 600 and 800 points for a singles game for 2–4 hours play. We recommend 800 points for 15mm singles tournament games (650 points for 25mm) and 1000 points for 15mm doubles games.

The army lists specify which troops can be used in a particular army. No other troops can be used. The number of bases of each type in the army must conform to the specified minima and maxima. Troops that have restrictions on when they can be used cannot be used with troops with a conflicting restriction. For example, troops that can only be used "before 450" cannot be used with troops that can only be used "from 450". All special instructions applying to an army list must be adhered to. They also apply to allied contingents supplied by the army.

All armies must have a C-in-C and at least one other commander. No army can have more than 4 commanders in total, including C-in-C, sub-commanders and allied commanders.

All armies must have a supply camp. This is free unless fortified. A fortified camp can only be used if specified in the army list. Field fortifications and portable defences can only be used if specified in the army list.

Allied contingents can only be used if specified in the army list. Most allied contingents have their own allied contingent list, to

Tlaxcalan with Captive

which they must conform unless the main army's list specifies otherwise.

BATTLE GROUPS

All troops are organised into battle groups. Commanders, supply camps and field fortifications are not troops and are not assigned to battle groups. Portable defences are not troops, but are assigned to specific battle groups.

Battle groups must obey the following restrictions:

- The number of bases in a battle group must correspond to the range specified in the army list.
- Each battle group must initially comprise an even number of bases. The only exception to this rule is that battle groups whose army list specifies them as 2/3 of one type and 1/3 of another, can comprise 9 bases if this is within the battle group size range specified by the list.
- A battle group can only include troops from one line in a list, unless the list specifies a mixed formation by specifying fractions of the battle group to be of types from two lines. e.g. 2/3 spearmen, 1/3 archers.
- All troops in a battle group must be of the same quality and training. When a choice of quality or training is given in a list, this allows battle groups to differ from each other. It does not permit variety within a battle group.
- Unless specifically stated otherwise in an army list, all troops in a battle group must be of the same armour class. When a choice of armour class is given in a list, this allows battle groups to differ from each other. It does not permit variety within a battle group.

EXAMPLE LIST

Here is a section of an actual army list, which will help us to explain the basics and some special features. The list specifies the following items for each historical type included in the army:

- Troop Type — comprising Type, Armour, Quality and Training.
- Capabilities — comprising Shooting and Close Combat capabilities.
- Points cost per base.
- Minimum and maximum number of bases in each battle group.
- Minimum and maximum number of bases in the army.

Aztec Calpolli Battle group

Troop name		Troop Type				Capabilities		Points per base	Bases per BG	Total bases
		Type	Armour	Quality	Training	Shooting	Close Combat			
Militia spearmen		Medium Foot	Protected	Average	Drilled	-	Light Spear, Swordsmen	7	6-8	12-56
				Poor				5		
Militia slingers		Light Foot	Unprotected	Average	Drilled	Sling	-	4	6-8	16-80
				Poor				2		
Inca noble guardsmen		Medium Foot	Protected	Superior	Drilled	-	Heavy Weapon	10	4-6	0-6
Cañari guardsmen	Only from 1490	Medium Foot	Protected	Superior	Drilled	-	Offensive Spearmen	10	4-6	0-6	0-10
Anti or Chuncho guardsmen		Light Foot	Unprotected	Superior	Drilled	Bow	-	6	2/3 6-9 / 1/3 4	0-4
		Medium Foot	Unprotected	Superior	Drilled	Bow	Swordsmen	8	4	

SPECIAL FEATURES:

- Militia spearmen must be organised in battle groups of 6 or 8 bases. They can be of Average or Poor quality. All the bases in a battle group must be of the same quality, but different battle groups can be of different quality. The list specifies the different points costs. The army must include at least 12 bases of militia spearmen and cannot include more than 56.
- Militia slingers must be organised in battle groups of 6 or 8 bases. They can be of Average or Poor quality. All the bases in a battle group must be of the same quality, but different battle groups can be of different quality. The list specifies the different points costs. The army must include at least 16 bases of militia slingers and cannot include more than 80.
- The Inca list (see page 53) has an additional special instruction: "The number of battle groups of Poor militia slingers cannot exceed the number of battle groups of Poor militia spearmen.", which is an additional restriction on top of those stated above.
- Inca noble guardsmen must be organised in a battle group of 4 or 6 bases. The total number of bases of Inca noble guardsmen in the army cannot exceed 6.

- Cañari guardsmen and Anti or Chuncho guardsmen can only be used from 1490 AD. Cañari guardsmen can either be organised in a battle group of 4 or 6 bases of Cañari guardsmen, or in a mixed battle group with Anti or Chuncho guardsmen comprising 4 bases of Cañari guardsmen and 2 bases of Light Foot Anti or Chuncho guardsmen or 6 bases of Cañari guardsmen and 3 bases of Light Foot Anti or Chuncho guardsmen. Anti or Chuncho guardsmen can either be organised in a battle group of 4 bases of Light Foot or Medium Foot Anti or Chuncho guardsmen, or in a mixed battle group with Cañari guardsmen as above. The total number of bases of Cañari guardsmen in the army cannot exceed 6. The total number of bases of Anti or Chuncho guardsmen in the army cannot exceed 4.

- The total number of bases of all types of guardsmen in the army cannot exceed 10.

Troop name	Troop Type				Capabilities		Points per base	Bases per BG	Total bases
	Type	Armour	Quality	Training	Shooting	Close Combat			
Separately deployed veteran warriors	Heavy Foot or Medium Foot	Protected	Superior	Undrilled	-	Impact Foot, Swordsmen	9	6-8	6-24
Warriors	Medium Foot	Protected	Average	Undrilled	Bow*	Impact Foot, Swordsmen	8	8-10	24-96
		Unprotected					7		
Skirmishers	Light Foot	Unprotected	Average	Undrilled	Javelins	Light Spear	4	6-8	6-24
	Light Foot	Unprotected	Average	Undrilled	Bow	-	5	6-8	

SPECIAL FEATURES:

- Separately deployed veteran warriors must be organised in battle groups of 6 or 8 bases. They can be Heavy Foot or Medium Foot, but all the bases in a battle group must be of the same type. The Eastern Woodland Culture list (see page 78) has an additional special instruction: "Separately deployed veteran warriors can be graded as Heavy Foot or Medium Foot but all separately deployed veteran warriors of the same tribe must be graded the same. Those of allied tribes can be graded differently." This means that all battle groups of separately deployed veterans in the main army must be graded the same, but those in an allied contingent can be graded differently. The army must include at least 6 bases of separately deployed veteran warriors and cannot include more than 24.

- Warriors must be organised in battle groups of 8 or 10 bases. They can be Protected or Unprotected. All the bases in a battle group must have the same armour level, but different battle groups can have different armour levels. The list gives the different points costs. The army must include at least 24 bases of warriors and cannot include more than 96.

- Skirmishers must be organised in battle groups of 6 or 8 bases. They can either have Javelins and Light Spear capabilities or Bow capability. All the bases in a battle group must have the same capabilities. The army must include at least 6 bases of skirmishers and cannot include more than 24.

APPENDIX 2 – THEMED TOURNAMENTS

A tournament based on the "Blood and Gold"
theme can include any of the armies listed in
this book.

Caonabo, Taíno chieftain, massacres Columbus' men, by Adam Hook. Taken from Warrior 40:
The Conquistador 1492–1550.

INDEX